RAND

Reinventing Public Education

Paul T. Hill

Supported by the
Lilly Endowment Inc. and the
George Gund Foundation

Institute on
Education and Training

RAND's Institute on Education and Training conducts policy analysis to help improve education and training for all Americans.

The Institute examines *all* forms of education and training that people may get during their lives. These include formal schooling from preschool through college; employer-provided training (civilian and military); post-graduate education; proprietary trade schools; and the informal learning that occurs in families, in communities, and with exposure to the media. Reexamining the field's most basic premises, the Institute goes beyond the narrow concerns of each component to view the education and training enterprise as a whole. It pays special attention to how the parts of the enterprise affect one another and how they are shaped by the larger environment. The Institute:

- examines the performance of the education and training system

- analyzes problems and issues raised by economic, demographic, and national security trends

- evaluates the impact of policies on broad, systemwide concerns

- helps decisionmakers formulate and implement effective solutions.

To ensure that its research affects policy and practice, the Institute conducts outreach and disseminates findings to policymakers, educators, researchers, and the public. It also trains policy analysts in the field of education.

RAND is a private, nonprofit institution, incorporated in 1948, which engages in nonpartisan research and analysis on problems of national security and the public welfare. The Institute builds on RAND's long tradition—interdisciplinary, empirical research held to the highest standards of quality, objectivity, and independence.

In 1991, RAND's newly established Institute on Education and Training (IET) invested in a study of alternative approaches to the governance of public education. The study's goal was to find ways of freeing teachers and principals from the heavy burden of regulation that reduced U.S. schools' productivity, while ensuring that schools remained accountable to the public. It was inspired by earlier research showing that site-based management and other "decentralization" efforts initiated by school systems had largely failed. Those efforts did not change the basic centralizing forces in school systems: school boards that create mandates affecting all schools, control of funding by the head office, and civil service rules and union contracts that determine teacher assignments and working conditions.

The study, which was funded by grants from the Lilly Endowment and the George Gund Foundation, focused on organizations that relied on the initiative of units in the field. It tried to identify the ways in which such organizations pursue corporate goals but maintain local initiative. This report applies the lessons drawn from such organizations to public education. It recommends a new approach to the governance of public education, based on contracts between local public education authorities and individual schools. The report shows in detail how a contracting system would work and how it can be established, replacing the entire existing public education governance system. It also shows why contracting is a workable alternative to the current system and why other alternatives, including education vouchers and "alignment" of the existing system under more explicit goals and standards, are not.

This report is written for people interested in dramatically improving the effectiveness of public education. Because educators are unlikely to change the system without major pressure and assistance from senior community and government leaders, this report speaks primarily to mayors, heads of business, community, and parent organizations, governors, state legislators, and school board members. It is also intended to help and encourage the thousands of people now working in public education who desperately want to make it work better, including teachers, principals, school superintendents, central office administrators, teacher union heads, and professors in schools of education.

Three other papers produced by the project are published separately: Bruce Bimber of RAND and the University of California, Santa Barbara, wrote *School Decentralization: Lessons from the Study of Bureaucracy*, RAND, MR-157-GGF/LE, 1993, and *The Decentralization Mirage*, RAND, MR-459-GGF/LE, 1994. Mary Beth Celio wrote *Building and Maintaining Systems of Schools: Lessons from Religious Order School Networks*, 1995 (forthcoming).

This is the first report issued by the Program on Reinventing Public Education, a collaboration between RAND's IET and the University of Washington's Institute for Public Policy and Management.

CONTENTS

Why has a decade of work on school reform produced so little? New programs, curricula, and accountability schemes, site-based management, and more money all appear to have little effect. Why is this so?

School governance is at least part of the answer. The very term is enough to make the eyes glaze over. It conjures up images of school boards meeting until midnight to decide whether to reroute a school bus, of administrators intent on measuring to the minute how long the school day should be, of bean counters tracking every dollar to its source, and of officials dedicated to upholding the letter of the law whatever its spirit.

As the adage holds, "The devil is in the details." The details of governance—how public officials supervise a school, how much discretion teachers and principals have, and how decisions are made about curriculum, teaching methods, student attendance, graduation requirements, hiring, and quality control—determine whether schools can change and improve. Unless new and better governance arrangements can be developed, the decade-long effort to reform American public education is doomed to failure.

Two theses are central to this report. First, the seeds of today's disappointments were sown when education reformers of the 19th century defined a public school as an institution financed, owned, and managed by a local agency of government. Second, public management of education has created a governance system divorced from public needs and democratic change, a system incapable of renewing itself.

American public schools have become government institutions, not community enterprises dedicated to the raising of children. They are buffeted by decisions made in the political arena, distracted from their instructional and nurturing missions by conflicts among adults, and hamstrung by regulations enacted in efforts to improve them. Schools may or may not need more money, better curricula, and better buildings. What is clear is that they now fail to make full use of the funds, equipment, and human talents already available to them.

Americans know what an effective school is, but we are unable to create them in great numbers. In surveys and focus groups across the country, people say they want schools in which

- Teachers know their material and present it well.

- Each child is led to learn and accomplish as much as he or she can.

- Students who fall behind or encounter problems get help; the school will not give up on a student.

- Children understand the importance of what they are taught.

- Parents know what their children are experiencing in school and why, and know that the staff consider parents to be partners, not adversaries.

- Adults in the school form personal relationships with children and assume responsibility for how well every child learns.

- Adults set good examples of fairness, honesty, and generosity.

Regrettably, the system of rules, supervision, and accountability by which we govern public education makes it difficult for schools to develop and sustain these characteristics. There are public schools with these qualities, but they almost always exist outside the mainstream and are tolerated as rare and deviant cases, not as models to be encouraged or emulated. The goal of governance reform is to build a system in which such schools are commonplace, not rare.

To date, all the efforts to reform governance of public education have been piecemeal. Voucher plans define how parents obtain the financial resources to demand better public schools, but not how public or private agencies will provide better schools. Charter schools reduce the burden of regulation on a few schools, but leave the vast majority under the existing governance system. Site-based management changes decisionmaking at the school level, but does nothing to change the mission and powers of the central office and little to minimize federal and state regulations, categorical program requirements, and union contract prohibitions. School board reformers urge an end to micromanagement, but they do not relieve board members of the need to resolve complaints and conflicts by making new policies that constrain all schools. "Systemic" reforms try to "align" the different parts of public education via mandated goals, tests, curriculum frameworks, and teacher certification methods, but do nothing to eliminate the political and contractual constraints that create fragmented, unresponsive schools.

None of these proposals offers a complete alternative to the existing governance system. They leave intact the core of the existing system: the commitment to governing public schools via politically negotiated rules that apply to all schools. Because most of the reforms now openly discussed in public forums can be gradually eroded by the creation of new rules, they are more likely to be transformed by the existing education governance system than to transform it.

THE GOAL OF THIS REPORT

The goal of this report is to formulate a true alternative to the current form of governance for public education. Based on studies of local educational reform efforts and of governance in other large decentralized service organizations, the report concludes that there is a real alternative. Unlike the current system, in which schools are both funded and operated by a government agency, the alternative allows schools to be operated by a variety of public and private organizations, based on school-specific contracts that would define each school's mission, guarantee public funding, and establish standards and procedures for accountability.

CONTRACTING: A NEW WAY OF GOVERNING PUBLIC SCHOOLS

Contracting builds on the charter schools movement (see Kolderie 1992; Nathan 1989), which permits groups to run publicly funded schools without following all the public school system's rules. Under a contracting system, every school would have a charter. A school board would not directly run schools, but would contract with independent organizations to run them. A local public school system would manage many different contracts, some for high schools and some for grade schools, some for highly distinctive schools (e.g., Montessori grade schools and high schools focused on health careers, great books, multicultural curricula, etc.) and others for more conventional schools. Every school's contract would specify the amounts of public funds it would receive, the type of instructional program it would provide, and the student outcomes it expects to produce.

The contract terms and the basic state licensing and student graduation requirements that now apply to all private schools would comprise the sole and entire method of public control over a school's curriculum and teaching methods. Contracting would require school boards to make educational decisions on a school-by-school basis, rather than by making policies that constrain all schools. In considering a particular contract, the school board need not ask whether a school concept is right for all or most of the students in the district, or whether some stakeholder groups would dislike a particular school. All the board would need to ask is whether there is a need for a particular school and whether the people proposing to run it have plausible credentials for doing so.

Public officials would retain ultimate responsibility for school quality. They could replace a contractor that failed to deliver, or force substantial quality improvements if performance in its schools fell below acceptable levels. A local school board could also continually "prune" its portfolio of contractors. When contracts came up for renewal, providers whose schools fell below some set level of performance could be eliminated from consideration. Contracting allows something that is not possible in public education today: unrelenting attention to the quality of instruction and learning in the lowest-performing schools.

Some contract schools could be run by the staff and parents of existing successful schools: neighborhood schools with good records of serving their students and communities, and magnet schools with well-defined programs and histories of success with average, as well as exceptional, students. Other school contracts could be established through the issuance of public requests for proposals, and still others might be negotiated directly with community groups or educational institutions that offer to run one or more schools.

The core purpose of contracting is to create schools that have clear missions and definite strategies for motivating students and delivering instruction. A school's contract would specify the goals it would seek and the methods it would use. A potential contractor could propose to establish a school with particular goals and methods. A local school board could also request proposals for a school that meets a defined need (e.g., emphasizing apprenticeship-style education) or an organized demand (e.g., emphasizing high academic standards and African culture and history).

Teachers would work for individual schools—as owner-operators, members of cooperatives, partners in a professional organization, or employees. Some teachers might form their own contracting organizations, and find teachers via their own professional networks. Contractors could also hire teachers through the local teacher union, which might operate as a guild hiring hall, brokering teachers into schools that fit them and suggesting additional training for teachers who have not been chosen by any school. Teacher salary scales would be set by the market, so that teachers with fine reputations could demand higher pay; some might also accept lower pay in order to work in highly attractive schools.

Each school's contract would specify processes and standards for student admission. To avoid charges of discrimination, all school contracts would call for admissions by random selection from the list of all who apply. No school would be allowed to handpick only the ablest students.

Schools would also be obligated to help students having academic difficulty, and to do everything possible to help students benefit from instruction. A school could set requirements about homework, attendance, and diligence, but it must continue helping students as long as they made the required effort.

Local school boards not wanting to execute separate contracts with dozens or hundreds of individual schools might prefer to deal with organizations capable of running several schools under a master contract. Organizations responsible for several schools, called Management and Assistance Providers (MAPs), could be a local board's prime contractors. MAPs could develop distinctive approaches to student instruction and staff training and capitalize on the recognition and consumer confidence that a "brand name" engenders.

Contracting has three major advantages. It

- Creates positive performance incentives for school staffs;
- Ensures that public funds are spent at the school level, where they count; and
- Deflects pressure for overregulation of schools.

Because contract schools would be schools of choice, a school would need to attract students in order to survive. It must therefore offer something that sets it apart—a distinctive curriculum, social climate, or extracurricular program. It must also provide a stable program that parents can rely on. Contracting therefore encourages a number of behaviors that "effective schools" advocates have tried to create in public school staffs. School staffs would have a strong incentive to set out a mission for the school and to ensure that all parts of the school work together.

Contracting creates strong pressures on public officials to maximize the share of funds spent at the school level and limit the amount spent on administration, regulation, and support of central decisionmaking processes. School contractors will know exactly how much money they have to spend, and therefore how much is skimmed off by the state or local central offices. Superintendents and boards will have to explain where money goes and why central office activities cost as much as they do.

Contracting would stabilize the rules under which schools operate. Public officials are now free to impose new requirements on schools at will: since nobody knows exactly how much money schools spend, or for what, it is hard to quantify the cost of a new mandate to add a course, write new reports, change staff assignments, or mainstream a group of students who were previously served in a special program. School contractors would be in a strong position to point out what new requirements cost and how they affect productivity.

CONCLUSION

Contracting is a promising idea that deserves a serious test. It could work for the vast majority of U.S. school systems. Any K–12 public education system that has more than one school can hold multiple contracts, one for each school. Even small-town and rural school systems with only one large high school could create two or more smaller schools within the same building, and benefit from the flexibility, diversity, and performance pressures that contracting provides.

Most of the important actors in public education would benefit from contracting. Public officials and taxpayers would know that funds for education were truly spent on schools, not bureaucracy. School boards that have struggled for years to improve particular schools could use contracts to restaff or recommission those schools. Teachers and administrators would gain the satisfaction of working in organizations that were free to be productive. Teachers who showed they could run successful schools would gain new professional opportunities, even including extra income.

School boards in the big cities can be the first to take advantage of the new opportunity by contracting out for operation of their lowest-performing schools. This would subject the concept to a hard first test. Success in the most difficult places will make the case for the widespread adoption of contracting.

ACKNOWLEDGMENTS

This report has one author, but it is the product of many minds. Georges Vernez, the IET's first director, suggested the study. He and his successor, Roger Benjamin, provided intellectual and financial support throughout. Susan Bodilly, Thomas Glennan, and Dean Millot of RAND commented on research plans and acted as critics and goads to the author. Bruce Bimber, Michael Mack, Kelly Warner, and Mary Beth Celio worked on the project and contributed papers used in the analysis; some of those papers are being published separately.

People in many cities submitted to interviews, allowed members of the study team to sit in on their deliberations, and listened patiently to presentations of preliminary findings. Special thanks are due to Ted Saunders and the staff of the Ohio Department of Education, David Bergholz of the George Gund Foundation, the Chicago school board, Barbara Holt of the Chicago School Finance Authority, Robert Wehling and Doris Holtzheimer of Procter and Gamble, Cincinnati Superintendent Michael Brandt, countless central office and school staff members in Cincinnati and Louisville, the Seattle Alliance for Education, members of the Seattle Powerful Schools Coalition, Sam Sperry of *The Seattle Post-Intelligencer*, Anne Hallett and other members of the Cross-City Coalition for School Reform, Christopher Cross of the Business Roundtable, Ted Kolderie, Jackie Dansberger, Michael Strembitsky, and Betty Jane Narver and numerous faculty members at the University of Washington's Graduate School for Public Affairs.

Reviewers Robert Palaich of the Education Commission of the States, Jane Hannaway of the Urban Institute, and James Harvey helped clarify the report and contributed important ideas.

The generous people named above are, however, not responsible for this report: its faults are the author's.

Chapter One

INTRODUCTION

Why does education reform have so little to show for a decade devoted to school improvement? Overall achievement is scarcely changed for the better, if at all. Dropout rates and serious disciplinary problems continue at extraordinary levels. New programs, new curricula, the addition of new money, accountability schemes, and site-based management—even the creation in many communities of pre- and after-school care and coordinated social services within the school—appear to have had little effect. Why is this so? Are the larger community difficulties in urban areas so intractable that schools, in the face of these problems, are helpless to influence student achievement? Or is something more subtle at work?

This report traces today's disappointments to two sources. The first is the definition of a public school as an institution financed, owned, and managed by civil servants employed by a local agency of government. The second source is public education's perverse system of governance, which isolates schools from public needs and democratic change. Overseen by distant government agencies, shaped by mandates from outside the schools and on top of them, driven by budgets they have no hand in developing, the professionals who administer and teach in public schools are preoccupied with compliance, not school effectiveness.

Many reform advocates criticize schools because they refuse to respond to pressures on them. That criticism is not entirely accurate. The school governance contraption behaves like foam rubber; "nerflike," it responds promptly to any and all pressures on it, and to pressures from many directions simultaneously. But when the pressure is removed, the contraption immediately reclaims its original shape.

Gridlock, a metaphor often used to characterize national government, describes decisionmaking in many school systems. Regulatory trucks block key intersections, judicial delivery vans double park wherever they choose, and conflicting signals from administrators, teachers, and politicians tie up educational traffic. As at the national level, gridlock leads to waste, confusion, and mediocrity.

The same is true within most schools. Public schools are expected to offend no one and to faithfully implement the settlement of every community dispute about how children should be taught and disciplined, what values should be honored or ignored, and how parents, teachers, and administrators should do business with one another. The result is that the work lives of many teachers and administrators are dominated by efforts to ensure that they and others comply with all applicable rules. One by one, the rules appear well conceived and benign. Collectively, they channel the efforts of teachers and administrators toward the bureaucratic activities of interpretation and negotiation, and away from the professional activities of instruction and adaptation to students' needs.

In the school systems RAND has studied over the past decade, virtually all school professionals, and the parents and community members who concern themselves with school quality, say that they would prefer a system that ran more on trust and respect for professional initiative. Yet few feel that they can rely on others to take reasonable initiatives, reciprocate concessions, or avoid taking advantage of weaknesses. Even the teachers who work together in particular schools often complain that many colleagues "work to rule," lecturing to their classes but contributing little to the overall climate of the school or efforts to improve it. Outside the schools, parent and community groups are often frustrated with school boards which, they report, cannot make clear decisions and stick with them. School board members, on the other hand, claim that it is almost impossible to reconcile the diverse demands made by parents, community groups, and employee unions.

School boards now act as little legislatures, receiving demands from all parts of the community and finding ways to respond, in some minimally acceptable way, to all of them. Like all legislatures, school boards handle demands through the processes of compromise and logrolling. When school boards reach compromises among competing demands, they encode the results in rules of general applicability that constrain how staff use time and solve problems. When school boards handle demands by logrolling, they also constrain the schools via specific directives about how particular issues or complaints are to be handled. The result, in either case, is to sustain what Tyack (1974, 1990) calls fragmented centralization, i.e., the control of the schools by multiple uncoordinated mandates and reporting requirements, not by comprehensive plans or designs.

Fragmented centralization is the worst of all possible worlds. Public education has neither the ideal centralized system's advantages of close coordination and rationalized procedures nor the ideal decentralized system's advantages of personal responsibility and problem solving close to the customer. No one gives orders, yet no one feels free to act decisively. Actors at all levels make work for one another and believe they could do their jobs better if the others would just get out of the way.

Our public school systems turn the business literature on Total Quality Management on its head. By strictly limiting the freedom and responsibility of the people on the front lines—principals and teachers—American public education puts apparent fairness and the avoidance of problems and controversy first and productivity second. If schools were problem-solving organizations, they would be diverse—as different as required in a society where children have different interests, gifts, language backgrounds, and degrees of academic preparation, and teachers have different talents. The fact they are, to the contrary, compliance organizations makes most of them passive, routinized, and slow to adapt to changes in students' needs, technology, and teacher talents.

A few school superintendents and teacher union leaders have tried to reform the system gradually and from within. To date, however, efforts to reform governance of public education have been piecemeal. Proposals to reform school boards and promote school site management within the existing system assume that people can change their behavior without clear incentives to do so. School board members are exhorted to forgo micromanaging and creating new policies in response to every problem. School staff are exhorted to take initiative even when the final decision about what they can do and how long they can do it rests with the school board and central office bureaucracy. Site-based management and efforts to reduce fragmented centralization by waiving selected regulations leave the core of current governance arrangements intact—the commitment to governing public schools with politically negotiated rules of general applicability and the mentality that "one size fits all." (See Bimber 1993; Hill and Bonan 1991.)

GOALS AND METHODS OF THIS REPORT

Can we find ways to govern schools so that conflicting rights and aspirations are respected, yet teachers and principals can focus on instruction, not compliance? This report tries to answer that question by developing and analyzing alternative governance arrangements.

Some have suggested that the governance problems of public education cannot be solved—that schools can be effective only if they are privately owned and operated. Others are convinced that simple privatization is no solution, because it does not answer the question of how society will protect children from possible harm or neglect at the hands of those who would educate them. As Elmore (1986) has shown, whatever the virtues of tuition tax credits and other forms of government support for private schools, they clearly do not eliminate the need for societal decisionmaking about how much will be spent on education, how minorities should be protected from discrimination, how children are to be protected from the negligence and mistaken notions of the adults responsible for their education, and what standards schools must meet to be eligible for public support.

The goal of the study that led to this report was to identify alternative forms of societal decisionmaking that would permit schools to be both democratically controlled and effective. The goal required imagining something that does not exist, i.e., a set of new approaches to public governance of schools, and anticipating the likely consequences of adopting each alternative.

The goal of formulating alternatives required unusual research methods. Because virtually all public school systems are governed by the same rules and processes, researchers had to derive alternatives from sources other than observation of public school systems. Three sources of ideas were available. The first source is theory: What do theories of democratic decisionmaking and public administration suggest? The second source drew on analogies: What approaches to governance are used by organizations that resemble public school systems in at least some ways? The third source was the experience of reformers hoping to change school governance in major cities: In places such as Chicago, Cincinnati, New York, and Detroit, what changes did reformers initiate? In light of their early experience, what can we learn about possible consequences in terms of local politics and the actions of teachers, administrators, and interest groups?

The reviews of theory examined management texts, business administration studies, theories of bureaucracy, and studies of innovation in public-sector organizations. The results are used throughout the rest of the report. The search for analogies consumed the lion's share of study resources. Researchers sought case studies of governance methods in organizations that resembled public school systems in four ways: they have definite corporate goals, including delivery of high-quality services; they deliver key services at many widely scattered locations; they require the use of specialized skills and knowledge by service deliverers; and they depend for their success on collaborative efforts of professionals at remote sites.

These criteria screen out many private-sector franchise organizations, such as True Value hardware stores or McDonald's restaurants, which maintain quality through detailed control of the whole service-delivery process. The criteria also eliminate independent schools and other single-site professional organizations, which can maintain quality and collaboration through direct personal contact. But the criteria admit a large number of organizations, including multisite law firms, the State Department, and the armed services, all of which seek definite corporate goals but depend on the initiative of professionals at remote locations. We also examined foreign and religious school systems, which face many of the same problems afflicting public school systems with regard to maintaining quality and fidelity to broader corporate purposes.

Like all analogies, these are imperfect. All the organizations listed above resemble public school systems in some ways and differ from them in others. The analogous organizations provide examples of alternative approaches to governance, which can be analyzed for their possible fit and utility in a public school context.

The third approach, analysis of the rudimentary governance reform efforts initiated by civic leaders in a few cities, was necessarily opportunistic. It was not possible to observe the implementation of a rich variety of educational governance approaches, because few serious efforts exist. Those that do are seriously handicapped by local political struggles. We were, however, able to work as participant observers in some of the most ambitious of these reforms, notably in Chicago, Cincinnati, and New York.

All of the reform efforts observed in the course of this study are still in midstream. None of the ideas we helped develop or that we analyzed has been fully implemented or tested. Our experiences produced only hypotheses and insights, not settled conclusions. They helped, however, to improve our understanding of the findings from the reviews of theory and analogous organizations.

The results of this study can only be ideas requiring further development and testing. However, the value of such ideas, to public school systems that tend to accept existing governance arrangements as the natural order of things, should not be underestimated.

THE PLAN OF THE REPORT

Under the original conception of the research project, this final report was to present several alternative forms of governance for big-city public school systems. As a result of what was learned during the course of the research, this report differs from expectations in two ways: First, it focuses on one alternative form of governance, contracting between local public education authorities and individual schools or groups of schools. It does so because contracting appears, as will be argued below, to be the only governance alternative that both dramatically reduces the burden of regulation on schools yet retains some form of public accountability. Second, the alternative form of governance presented is meant to apply to the vast majority of U.S. school systems, large or small. Contracting can, with a few modifications, be applied to virtually any school system large enough to have more than one school.

The remainder of the report consists of five chapters. Chapter Two makes the basic case that our present governance system in urban schools is failing. Chapter Three is an overview of the existing governance arrangements in urban public education, linking many of the failures of the schools to the governance structure. Chapter Four sketches an alternative governance system based on contracts between local public authorities and schools or groups of schools. Chapter Five analyzes two other widely discussed alternative forms of governance—one based on total privatization of ownership and control of schools, and one based on rigorously aligned performance standards, testing, and teacher training—and shows how they are distinctly inferior to contracting. Chapter Six suggests how states and local communities can move toward contracting and how state and federal governments can promote local governance reforms.

Chapter Two

THE PROBLEM

Almost nobody is content with America's public school systems, least of all the people who work in them. Teachers asked to describe the kind of school they prefer to work in talk about much more orderly, focused, and collaborative work environments than they currently encounter. Principals, superintendents, school board members, and teacher union leaders each claim that they could work more effectively with less interference from the others. Business leaders uniformly disparage the skills of school graduates. Many parents are satisfied if the school is thought to be safe, but most worry about the quality of education their children receive. Students demonstrate their contempt for the education provided to them by dropping out in droves without diplomas.

Conservative critics charge that schools have lowered their standards to accommodate the needs of the disadvantaged. The position that "schools must stop putting equity above quality" encapsulates their argument. It appears indisputably true that school standards have fallen, but they have not fallen to the benefit of poor and minority students, who are failing in ever-increasing numbers. They have fallen across the board: According to international comparisons, the performance of the best mathematics students in the United States, i.e., the top 5 percent, is about equal to the performance of average students in many other nations.

Nobody would consciously set out to design the kinds of governance arrangements characteristic of schools today in the United States. But these arrangements developed by accretion, without a great deal of thought, and slowly over time. They were hardly deliberately de-signed at all.

In many ways, the general public and the people who administer public education have only themselves to blame for the sorry state of schools today. Certainly, neither would have put up with outsiders imposing today's governance arrangements on the schools. In the words of an immortal American philosopher, Pogo, "the enemy is us": The sensible idea that schools should be accountable to public needs has had the practical effect of shaping day-to-day governance in the image of the political arena. With the political arena's shape come its goals—satisfying as many as possible, injuring as few as possible, protecting traditional constituents, and responding to new claims as they arise—and its reliance on politically negotiated set-tlements, deal making, and logrolling.

When the public thinks of schools, political bargaining is not the first image that springs to mind. In public, education officials almost never speak about the political dimensions of their work; in private, they rarely speak of anything else. In the lobbies and restaurants of hotels hosting education meetings, late-night discussions are domi-nated by political talk in its broadest sense—pressure from a board member to find a job for a relative, the colleague caught with a hand in the cookie jar, outrageous pressure from one interest group or an-other, the school calendar held hostage to buses and local teamsters, taxpayer resentment of school budgets, and the latest lawsuits in which individuals, schools, districts, or states are engaged.

Local politics are played out in many districts, not only in the broad-est sense of legitimate democratic pressures on the schools, but also in the narrowest, partisan sense of the schools as a significant ele-ment in local patronage networks. A former teacher in Pennsylvania told a Villanova University researcher:

> I used to be a teacher . . . . When I got here I was told that the job was totally political. They told me that I would have to register to vote, and get the application from my political committeeman. You get discouraged when things like that happen—I decided I didn't want to be a teacher in this kind of system.

The effort to govern schools through political bargaining inevitably makes them the focus of community conflict—about values, individual morality, civic responsibility, respect for minority needs, and the imperative to distribute economic opportunity. Resolution of these conflicts—through negotiation, the creation of group rights, and straightforward horse trading—creates the procedures and their accompanying regulations that shape the conduct of today's schools. And these threaten daily to displace the goal at the center of schooling: producing competent graduates.

Americans quite properly seek public schools that both respect the rights and values of a diverse population and make the most of the talents and initiative of individual students and teachers. Unfortunately, the rules, regulations, and bureaucratic machinery created to attend to the first of these goals threatens to overwhelm the second. The result: a system that hardly works at all and works well for very few.

THE MEANING OF PUBLIC EDUCATION, AND OF GOVERNANCE

The term "public education" is widely used but seldom carefully defined. It certainly includes all forms of instruction in schools operated and funded from tax revenues by local public school boards. But there are many instances in which activities that people call public education lack one or more features of the foregoing definition. Public education students frequently receive instruction outside of publicly owned school buildings—at museums, concert halls, theaters, zoos, and public and private colleges and universities. Some public education services are also delivered by independent organizations, including private providers of special education and remedial services, language, science, and mathematics courses and enrichment, and public and private colleges. Some public education services are also funded entirely or in part through private donations, fundraising, and parental payments for extracurricular activities and instruction. Public school boards also place some handicapped students in privately managed facilities and pay tuition, and some privately run alternative schools are funded entirely through contracts with public school boards.

As these examples illustrate, public education is diverse, and the boundaries between it and private education are porous. Reduced to its lowest terms, public education is education authorized by local school boards and other instrumentalities of the state, fulfilling their responsibilities under state law. Subject to the provisions of state and federal laws and court orders (defining student eligibility for free public education, the rights of students, and the rights and obligations of teachers and administrators), any arrangements that duly constituted local school boards make for the education of children can be considered public education.

How is this amorphous enterprise governed? For the purposes of this report, "public education governance" is broadly defined to include all institutions that make education-related decisions: what goals publicly supported education is to meet, what institutions may deliver public education, how schools and other institutions are to be administered, who is to take part in internal decisionmaking and what roles they are to play, which students can receive public education, who may instruct students, what funds and other resources schools and other institutions will have, what services teachers and others must provide, how resources and services must be allocated among students, what courses students must take, and what students must be able to demonstrate before they can be recognized as graduates. The list of decisions to be made about public education, and of actors who take part in the decisions, is vast. A map of relevant decisions and actors would also illustrate the many potential roadblocks to school improvement. Not one of the agencies, actors, or power centers that make decisions about public education is, by itself, capable of improving a single school. They must all work together. But any one of them alone can stop reform dead in its tracks.

The most obvious sources of prescriptions about public education are the laws and regulations enacted by Congress, state legislatures, and state and local school boards. But those are simply the tip of the iceberg. In many localities, court orders determine how much schools will spend, whether students will attend school in their own neighborhoods or elsewhere for racial balance, what services parents of children with disabilities can demand, and whether or not local districts can offer special programs for particular kinds of youngsters with particular needs, e.g., young African American males. In many places, especially big cities, labor contracts—not only with teachers but also with administrators and custodians—determine when schools will open and close, who will administer them, who will teach in them, and the limits of adult responsibility.

The history of federal aid to elementary and secondary education illustrates the effects of simply one of these elements of public education governance. Decades of research reveal that educators are averse to enforcement and litigation and will do almost anything to avoid being dragged into court or an administrative hearing (Hannaway 1993). For over 20 years there were questions about the efficacy of the "pullout" method of service delivery, and federal officials repeatedly stated that pulling students out of their regular classrooms to receive supplementary instruction was not the only permissible way of delivering Chapter 1 services. But many states (e.g., Ohio) adopted their own policies requiring "pullouts," expressly choosing to limit service options rather than risk conflicts over legality. Even in states that did not follow Ohio's lead, the vast majority of school systems relied on the pullout method because it was the only one that never led to adverse findings by monitoring agencies.

GOVERNANCE AND QUALITY

Studies of American public education reveal three kinds of evidence to support the proposition that current governance arrangements militate against school quality: the difficulty of reproducing tested, effective innovations; inability to focus resources on schools in trouble; and tolerance for consistent failure. Any of these alone is cause for concern. Combined, they are a condemnation of current governance arrangements.

Success a Lonely Exception

Effective practice is difficult to reproduce in public schools. Something about the very nature of schools and their organization short-circuits the reform impulse, as the President of the United States recognized in May 1993 when honoring some 200 exemplary schools. "One of the most continually frustrating things I ever faced as governor [of Arkansas]," said President Clinton, "was realizing that virtually every challenge in American education has been met successfully by somebody, somewhere, [but] the problem is that we have never found an effective way to help replicate success."

It would be hard to put the governance problem of public education more succinctly. Although there are hundreds of examples of effective public schools—in urban, rural, and suburban neighborhoods—that provide rigorous instruction and help students succeed despite poverty and neighborhood problems, these schools are *always* treated as exceptions. Such schools are always "special" in some way: they have foundation grants, strong business support, or a warrant from the local school board to act as magnets delivering specialized instructional programs. Many such schools also have high-energy principals who can work around the central office bureaucracy or intimidate it, gain access to needed resources, and find teachers to complement those in the school. Nevertheless, the very fact that such schools are considered exceptional provides the rationale for other public schools to ignore them. The conventional wisdom that an excellent public school requires a charismatic leader or support from outside the education community is, in itself, tacit admission that the current governance structure is hostile to quality.

Schools that gain fine reputations are admired and heavily publicized, but school systems seldom do much more than go through the motions of trying to reproduce them. The annual spectacle of lines of parents camping overnight in line to enroll children in popular magnet schools exemplifies this problem. Public school systems can create good schools, but few systems see it as their job to duplicate success or to create for all schools the conditions that enable some schools to succeed.

Many systems seek help from educational innovators such as Theodore Sizer of Brown University, James Comer of Yale, or Henry Levin of Stanford. These innovators work with individual schools, often with striking results in terms of teacher and student effort and performance, and strong parent-school relations. But these schools function just like locally developed magnets—as exceptions, not as models for general improvement. Like the "Potemkin villages" that were spruced up to hide rural poverty from the eyes of the touring Russian czar, innovative schools are often used to create an impression of progress in a system where most schools are, in fact, mired in a bog of routine and failure.

Inability to Focus Resources on Problems

Another indicator of governance problems is that school systems seldom have any free resources to invest in major improvements or to intervene in desperately failing schools.

Competition for resources has created an overconstrained system, in which every dollar is spoken for, most allocated to teacher salaries or existing programs. New funds, e.g., from tax levy increases, are earmarked before they arrive, often to fund deferred maintenance, to roll back increases in average class size, or to finance commitments to increase staff salaries.

Even supposedly flexible categories of funds, such as staff development, are committed in advance, to separate categorical programs or to programs selected by central office administrators. In fact, in many cities the largest amounts of money available for staff development are set aside for salary increases to teachers who have taken additional university coursework. These funds are allocated unilaterally by teachers, who decide what courses interest them. Schools, supposed to be responsible for self-improvement, seldom have any capacity to influence teachers' decisions.

Some idea of the scale and scope of American education indicates why financial gridlock is a significant issue. The school system is always one of the largest employers in a major metropolitan area. As a nationwide enterprise, education spends more money and employs more people than the American automobile, steel, and textile industries combined. In any of those industries or any other sector of the private economy, managers routinely expect to be able to free up resources to respond to significant problems as they emerge. Very few school administrators have the same expectation.

Tolerance for Failure

The most devastating indicator of governance problems is that consistent failure is normal. It has come to be accepted, even tolerated. As one state superintendent has said, "The fact that we are in charge of the system and haven't been able to do anything to eliminate consistent and conspicuous failures means that we just don't have what it takes to do our job."

Most school systems of any size have schools in which dropout rates and other indicators of student failure have been unacceptably high for decades. Some of these schools have suffered consistent neglect, but many have been objects of repeated improvement programs. Most of these schools, in fact, contain large numbers of specialized instructional programs, counseling and self-esteem interventions, intensive health care programs, and even day care for students' babies.

The persistence of failure, despite turnovers in superintendents, school boards, and central office staff, indicates that the lack of capacity is not a leadership issue or a problem of personnel. The nature of the problem is systemic. As this report went to press, a new analysis of conflict within public schools was released by the Public Agenda Foundation (Farkas 1993). Based on focus group interviews in four school districts, the report concluded that "something about the system" is askew:

> We are discouraged by what we found. In each district, what started as a good-faith effort to work together on school reform became a tug-of-war over turf. We observed poor communication, widespread suspicion and outright anger among the factions. Parochialism prevailed.

> Because this pattern of behavior was so consistent in ... diverse school districts, we can only conclude that it was not the individuals but something about the system itself that encouraged conflict, not cooperation.

Public school systems are unable to find or develop the capabilities essential to their most fundamental task, offering high-quality schooling for the entire community. The system needs to change, but the barriers to reform are very strong. Reform requires a mixture of intellectual and political development. Reformers need more than a strong case against the current system: they need one or more coherent and workable alternatives, conceptions of a system that would be both accountable to the public and more conducive to effective schooling. This report seeks to create that alternative conception of public education.

Chapter Three

CURRENT GOVERNANCE AND ITS CONSEQUENCES

The current system of governance can be understood in terms of the ways in which it resolves certain key issues:

- **Definition.** What is it about a school that makes it public?

- **Organizing learning.** How is learning organized in the school? Who decides what is taught, who teaches, and how schools are staffed? How are students assigned to schools?

- **Initiative.** Do adults in individual schools have the initiative to tailor instruction to students? Do they take responsibility for results?

- **Resources and constraints.** How do schools get funds and resources? Are resources allocated fairly and consistently? Are the schools subject to abrupt and frequent changes in funding and in the rules under which they operate?

- **High performance.** What pressures from the state and from within the district encourage high performance in schools? How are students protected from school failure, and how are failing schools improved?

DEFINITION OF A PUBLIC SCHOOL

As Chapter Two demonstrated, the terms "public school" and "public education" are highly elastic. They are, however, most often used in one way, to refer to a school founded, owned, financed, and operated by a local government agency. The vast majority of students attend such schools. With remarkably few exceptions, new schools operate under the same policies and guidelines as those that already exist. They are, in effect, franchises, new manifestations of an existing model. On occasion, schools are created from scratch to serve special purposes, e.g., to educate students with specific handicaps or gifts, supply workers for a particular career, or serve as magnets for students interested in a specific academic curriculum. These schools typically attract students from a wide geographic area, but special-purpose schools typically comprise 5 percent or less of all the schools in a district.

Funding from public schools comes from many sources. Most local education agencies have their own sources of income from local property taxes, and many possess their own taxing authority. All local education agencies receive a substantial amount of money from state government. The average state contribution, about 50 percent, just about equals the average local contribution, but the state contribution varies widely from between 20 and 80 percent of total per-pupil expenditures. Small amounts (usually less than 10 percent) also come from the federal government, under formula-driven programs that target funding for special services to low-income, low-achieving, handicapped, or limited-English-speaking children. Foundation grants and discretionary awards from state and federal governments seldom amount to 1 percent of any local school system's income.

A significant amount of the funds available to school systems is spent outside the schools. All but the smallest rural school systems have complex central offices dedicated to accounting, purchasing, auditing, monitoring school compliance with mandates and court orders, hiring teachers, analyzing school and student performance, and providing technical assistance to teachers and schools. These offices can be large in absolute terms—New York City's, the largest, employs nearly 6,000 people, approximately six for every school. Though some analysts claim that urban systems spend more than half their funds outside the schools (Cooper 1993), the most thorough analyses estimate between 10 and 20 percent (Booz-Allen & Hamilton 1992).

Though most funds come to school systems on a student per-capita basis, schools do not get funded that way. Schools are not funded, but "resourced." Local school boards create formulas that determine, separately for grade schools and high schools, the number of teachers and administrators a school is entitled to claim. As Cooper (1993) has shown, a school is guaranteed a baseline level of administrative personnel, typically a principal, assistant principal, and secretary, and gains additional administrators with each increment of approximately 150 students. Schools typically also gain an additional teacher for each (roughly) 20 students, although the exact number varies from city to city. Schools also obtain desks, furniture, lab equipment, and other capital assets on a rough formula basis. Paper, books, and other instructional materials are allocated by formula. Repairs, remodeling, and utility bills are usually allocated and paid for by the school system.

In light of the huge amounts spent on education nationally, newcomers to education are often surprised to discover that relatively little cash actually reaches any school. School principals frequently administer small discretionary budgets, normally in the range of $30–$75 per student, to be used for paper, copying, activities, field trips, minor repairs, and hiring consultants and speakers. Most principals, when asked about the budget for their school, respond in terms of their discretionary account, not the entire amount required to operate the school, including funds for teacher salaries, supplies, and repairs. That explains why, in the course of four years of RAND field work—although the real annual operating costs of a city high school can range up to $10 million or more, and are rarely less than $1 million—no principal ever claimed to have a budget over $90,000.

Even federal and state categorical funds reach the schools in the form of specific resources, not flexible cash. In most districts, the central office hires a group of teachers who will be paid from funds from a specific grant, and allocates them to schools according to the funding source program's rules. School principals and regular instructional staff may be able to request supplementary teachers with particular training, but the assignments such teachers can accept within the school—what subjects and students they can teach and where—are determined by the funder's regulations and district policy.

ORGANIZING LEARNING

American school systems are also remarkably uniform in their decisionmaking on curriculum, teaching methods, and staffing.

Curriculum

Public school curricula are determined through public, often political, decisionmaking. State education agencies, operating under legislative guidance, set requirements for the length of the school year, credits required for high school graduation, and teacher and principal certification. Most state agencies also review textbooks and limit the texts that schools can use; larger states like California, New York, and Texas often commission their own textbooks. Since the late 1970s, many states have also designed minimum competency tests for high school graduation and publish curriculum guidelines identifying topics to be covered in courses. A separate state agency, the state higher education system, also influences high school curriculum by setting requirements for admission to state colleges and universities.

In theory, such state mandates are meant to ensure high-quality and professional oversight of local school systems. Many key decisions are in fact made by blue-ribbon panels made up of such groups as teachers, university professors, and employers. But many decisions are made or influenced through political processes, whether in the state legislature itself or in negotiations among interest groups. Several state legislatures, for example, have responded to popular discontent about education by imposing new standards and mandates without allowing for their cost. One state's "omnibus reform bill" was drafted by legislative staff under instructions to pick out the best ideas from several national reports, with the constraint that none could increase state funding for education. Moreover, many curriculum reform efforts have been forums for contention among interest groups about the content of multicultural curricula, the definition of sexist language, and the need to give equal attention to the histories and views of all groups.

Politics in such situations is neither good nor bad; it is inevitable. When decisions about the education of millions of children are centralized in one legislature or task force, agreement often can come only through the search for an inoffensive middle ground, trading off to ensure that each group gets as much as possible of what it wants and that irreconcilable differences are split. From the perspective of public schools, however, such actions at the state level constitute powerful constraints on what can be taught and how students' needs can be met.

Local school boards also have an impact on what gets taught and how. School boards can narrow schools' choices among the alternatives set by the state, designating just one textbook or set of filmstrips and workbooks. Local boards vary from the highly prescriptive—requiring that all teachers of a given subject cover materials in the same sequence and on the same schedule—to the permissive, encouraging schools to make any decision allowable under the state guidelines.

Teaching

Local school boards can also have a strong effect on how teachers teach. They, and the central office administrators who work under their direction, establish methods and standards for teacher evaluation and determine what kinds of in-service training teachers will attend. School boards also affect pedagogy in the way they resolve everyday conflicts and scandals. School boards are frequently asked to decide whether a particular way of grouping students constitutes discrimination, whether a teacher may punish or evict unruly students from her class, and whether all students have fair access to valued instructional programs. The cumulative effect of such decisions is to give teachers a quite detailed picture of what they must and must not do in the classroom. Though teachers are nominally free to devise and select their own methods, all operate under similar, and heavy, constraints. As in many other areas, the imperative of maintaining peace among adult interest groups drives instruction.

School boards also affect teaching in the process of collective bargaining with local teacher unions. Though most state laws prohibit collective bargaining over instructional issues, they do allow it over working conditions. Because working conditions include working hours, maximum class sizes, nonteaching duties, and teacher evaluation methods, collective bargaining can have a profound effect on how schools and classrooms are run. As McDonnell and Pascal (1988) have shown, school boards made major concessions on working conditions in the 1980s, when they could not afford to meet union salary demands. The result, in the majority of states that permit teacher collective bargaining, is that the teacher union is a virtual partner with the school board, determining who will teach whom, for how long, and to what standards. These practices set patterns followed throughout the country, even in districts that do not formally bargain with teacher unions.

School Staffing

To teach in a public school, a person must be qualified under guidelines set by the state. These normally require graduation from an accredited four-year college or university and completion of prescribed courses on teaching methods. Some states also require basic skills competency tests for all teachers and more specialized examinations for teaching science, mathematics, or English. These guidelines are broad and identify a large pool of potential teachers.

But if the state certifies teachers, it is local school systems that hire and fire them. Applicants with the formal qualifications set by the state apply to local school systems, which can reject them, hire them for full-time work, or put them on a list of eligible temporary or substitute teachers. The teacher hiring and placement system is indistinguishable from civil service hiring and placement procedures at the federal, state, or local levels. It is generally accompanied by all the benefits of such a system, including protection against blatant patronage and politically motivated efforts to fire personnel. And it has all the drawbacks of such a system, including inability to reallocate personnel swiftly as staffing needs change.

Significantly, it is the school system that hires the teacher, not an individual school. Under most board policies and collective-bargaining agreements, specific vacancies are filled by new hires only if no teacher currently working in the school system has claimed the job. In general, junior teachers have virtually no choice about where they will teach, and senior teachers have a great deal.

In recent years, the most important teacher assignment decisions have been prompted by declining enrollments and fiscal cutbacks, and very few members of the public are conscious of the staggering effect this may have on school operations. If a school's enrollment declines during the school year, it can lose teachers. Schools in the poorest areas, with the highest rates of student absenteeism, transience, and dropout, are most often affected. Inner-city high schools can lose 10 percent of their teachers or more in early January, when midyear enrollment figures are assembled. When this process starts, it launches a civil-service-like procedure of "bumping rights" based on seniority, a procedure that rumbles throughout the school system.

Teachers who leave a school (or administrators with teaching certificates who are removed from their central office jobs) need to find work elsewhere, and they do so on the basis of seniority. A teacher qualified to teach a particular grade or course can "bump" an incumbent. The bumping chain can be long, and it ends only when the last person bumped is too junior to possess any bumping rights. Financial cutbacks such as those recently experienced in most big cities can create massive bumping frenzies, often involving administrators who fled the classroom years ago. These are so disruptive to schools that boards and superintendents hesitate to add to organizational tension by suggesting teacher layoffs.

Early retirement plans are frequently offered, as they have been recently in Washington, D.C. Local airwaves pulse, as they did in Washington, with reassurances from superintendents and board members that announced reductions in teaching and administrative positions do not really mean what they appear to mean, because retirements and reassignments will protect most people. Teacher unions often cooperate in this effort by accepting furloughs for all teachers, rather than layoffs for some, and agreeing to almost any economy other than "increasing class size," i.e., laying off teachers.

One result of the seniority system is that the staffs of many schools are assembled through formal allocative processes, not at the initiative of the incumbent staff or principal. Though some senior teachers choose to work in the most demanding inner-city schools, most can avoid doing so if they wish. The result, in virtually all big cities, is that senior teachers cluster around "desirable" schools in low-stress, safe, middle-class areas. As the Los Angeles court case *Rodriguez* v. *Anton* has shown, this means that schools in the poorest areas, with the most unstable populations, are left with a disproportionate share of the youngest, least experienced, and, frequently, least qualified teachers.

Procedures for assignment of teachers and administrators emphasize equity for adults, but they reduce school flexibility. Senior teachers can decide where they will work regardless of whether they fit the school's needs. Literally every public school principal interviewed in five years of RAND research on urban schools complained about deadwood senior teachers who did not fit the school or sympathize with the problems of the students, but would not leave. Rapid student turnover is part of the problem: Within the working lives of older teachers, many urban school populations have turned over completely, from white to African American, and often again to Hispanic.

In cities like Houston, Los Angeles, and Miami, which have large immigrant populations, the dominant ethnicity and language of a school's student body can change completely within three years. In those cities, some teachers expressed hostility to "those kids" who had turned a familiar situation on its head, requiring changes in pedagogy that teachers were unwilling to make (McDonnell and Hill 1993).

Teacher assignment has a powerful impact on resource allocation. Under the district's allocation formula, a school has a certain number of slots for certified teachers, and it does not matter whether they are the most or least senior of the eligible individuals. A school can have all senior teachers (making, on the average of big-city systems, in excess of $55,000 per year) or all entry-level teachers (making on average barely $20,000), and the school system's accounting practices cannot tell the difference.

Student Assignment

Almost all students are assigned to schools based on where they live. It is an American tradition that students should attend school in their own neighborhoods whenever possible. In urban areas it is almost universally true that students attend elementary classes in their own neighborhoods, although their older siblings may have to travel much further to their middle or secondary school. Even at the elementary level, however, there are important exceptions to the general practice.

Some students in major urban areas are bused out of their neighborhood attendance zones for purposes of racial integration. Individual students are also allowed to attend schools outside their neighborhoods for purposes of special education or to take part in unusual instructional programs, e.g., at a science and mathematics or performing arts magnet school. School systems occasionally develop magnet schools in order to keep middle class students who might otherwise leave for private schools, or to create oases of integrated education in a school system that is geographically divided by race.

Though public school systems occasionally relax the connection between residence and school assignment for reasons of their own, they do so only reluctantly. Most are particularly reluctant to grant parents' requests to move from one school to another. If parents want a child to attend a school outside the neighborhood, they must often make the case that the local school lacks some program the child needs. Parents' requests are frequently denied if a transfer would adversely affect the racial balance of the sending or receiving school.

When families relocate, even within the same school system, children normally change schools. Midyear transfers can have a dramatic effect on the population of a school: Many schools in low-income and immigrant urban neighborhoods experience more than a 100 percent annual student turnover. Occasionally, these students move only a few blocks, continuing to believe they live in the same "neighborhood," but they are forced to transfer.

LOCUS OF INITIATIVE

A school system exists to provide education. Whether its governance system is good or bad depends entirely on whether it enables schools to do for children what parents and the broader community desire, which is to prepare them to become competent and productive adults.

On one level, Americans are deeply divided about what makes a good school. Debates about curriculum can become acrimonious enough to shatter a community, as recently happened in South Carolina, or to end the tenure of a powerful and otherwise popular school superintendent, as recently happened in New York City.

The intensity of such debates obscures a broad consensus about school purposes. The elements of this consensus, indeed, all came together in 1992, when the New American Schools Development Corporation (NASDC) solicited new school designs from educators, parent groups, community organizations, and private entities across the country. Although the 686 proposals received by NASDC differed dramatically on the details of curriculum, pedagogy, staff development, and use of technology, they were remarkably consistent about the nature of the core relationships that define a good school. These were:[1]

- Teachers know their material and present it well.

- Each child is led to learn and accomplish as much as he or she can.

- Students who fall behind or encounter problems get help; the school will not give up on a student.

- Children understand the importance of what they are taught.

- Parents know what their children are experiencing in school and why, and know that the staff consider parents to be partners, not adversaries.

- Adults in the school form personal relationships with children and assume responsibility for how well every child learns.

- Adults set good examples of fairness, honesty, and generosity.

Taken together, these characteristics form a somewhat old-fashioned view of a good school—a community institution in which educated adults pass on knowledge to children whom they know and care about as individuals. The entire concept is encapsulated in an African proverb quoted by dozens of NASDC proposals: "It takes a whole village to raise a child."

This simple and striking vision is rarely realized. As many recent anthropological studies have documented, public schools, especially

---

[1]These summaries build on an analysis of NASDC proposals conducted by Thomas K. Glennan of RAND.

the ones in the big cities, run more like branches of big government bureaucracies than like caring village centers.

Good schools are problem-solving organizations that use the talents and resources of the whole staff for every student. The school's mission also sets up high expectations for students. The school's promises, about what students will encounter while in the school and what they can do upon leaving it, are matched with demands about what the student must do to succeed. Teachers and administrators are not afraid to make demands on students. On the contrary, they assume that students need to work, and that the demands of a rigorous school can put meaning and structure into students' lives. These schools make demands on even the most disadvantaged students by demonstrating the rewards of hard work, not, as is too frequently the case, by treating them with the condescension of leniency. Such schools ultimately succeed because their vision of students' needs and adult responsibilities makes adults self-critical and demanding of one another. They are genuine enterprises, in which every member has an opportunity to succeed and the responsibility to help others do so as well. (See Hill, Foster, and Gendler 1990.)

Such schools are possible only if the people in them have the capacity to work effectively. That capacity depends on whether they have access to needed resources and the freedom to use those resources imaginatively.

RESOURCES AND RULES: FAIR AND STABLE

School finance reform is a well-established focus of educational policy debate. A series of books from Arthur Wise's *Rich Schools Poor Schools* (1968) through Jonathan Kozol's *Savage Inequalities* (1992) demonstrate the immense funding discrepancies between schools in wealthy communities and those serving low-income populations accompanied by weak property-tax bases.

Until recently, however, school finance reform has concentrated on within-state inequalities. Few school finance reform lawsuits have addressed funding inequalities within local school systems. These inequities are inevitably a consequence of local governance processes. State-level litigation has supported big-city and poor rural school systems' efforts to increase their gross income. It has ignored the fact, demonstrated in such local lawsuits as *Hobson* v. *Hansen* and *Rodriguez* v. *Anton*, that schools suffer most directly from the results of local governance processes creating vast resource inequalities between schools and forcing schools to adapt to ever-changing levels of staffing and funding.

Iniquities in local resource allocation interfere with the operation of responsible, problem-solving schools in three ways. First, they create such low levels of funding in some schools that their staffs have great difficulty delivering a high-quality program. Second, they weaken staff members' sense of personal responsibility by providing a ready excuse for low performance, i.e., the school is entitled to more resources. Third, they force continuous shifting of staff members and other resources from school to school, making it nearly impossible for school leaders to deliver stable programs or hold anyone responsible for the results.

Low Real Resources

Resource disparities within school systems are masked by the summary figures used to describe resource levels. Systemwide per-pupil expenditure figures do not describe every school's actual funding. Even after adjusting for expenditures on central office functions, per-pupil spending averages are misleading.

Within some local public school systems, the between-school differences in per-pupil expenditures can differ by 100 percent or more. Three factors lie at the root of the funding differences. First, school boards make conscious decisions to spend more on particular schools, e.g., to create lower student/teacher ratios in junior highs than in grade schools, or to provide extra aides for schools serving large numbers of special education students. Overcrowding is a second contributor: due to immigration or other population movements, some schools become overcrowded, badly distorting student/teacher ratios and other measures of resource concentration. The third factor was discussed above: senior teachers, who have first call on teaching vacancies, tend to avoid "problem" schools in turbulent low-income areas. Because senior teachers are often paid more than twice as much as junior ones, school systems can wind up spending nearly twice as much per pupil in some schools as in others.

These inequalities affect schools' real capabilities. Better-staffed high schools are bought at the cost of less well-staffed elementary schools. Overcrowded schools or those with very high student/teacher ratios have less opportunity to deliver imaginative and flexible instructional programs. Schools hamstrung with large numbers of inexperienced teachers, including teachers with provisional certificates because they have failed key courses or examinations, are inevitably less capable than schools with concentrations of better-trained and more experienced teachers.

Resource Instability

In the past decade, many school systems have experienced constant reallocation of their resources. The worst cases occurred in Los Angeles, Chicago, and New York, where declines in state and local revenues forced midyear reductions, often as great as 10 percent, in overall system budgets. But even in cities with stable total funding, student population movement forced continual frequent midstream changes in school staffing.

In most local systems, schools receive an initial allocation of staff members in September, when the first counts of school enrollments are available. These numbers are typically adjusted in October, when student attendance figures start to fall due to dropouts, transfers, and low daily attendance rates. Surprisingly, the figures are often adjusted again in January and March. In some high schools, the only thing certain about teacher assignment is that no student will have the same teacher for longer than one semester at a time.

Turbulent resource allocation obviously interferes with a school's ability to deliver consistent programs and to take responsibility for the progress of individual students. Clearly it destroys any relationships formed between students and teachers. To support the kinds of high-quality schools discussed above, school systems must be capable of stabilizing their schools, either by guaranteeing fixed minimum staffing levels despite student turnover, or by permitting students to remain in the same school even when they move to new neighborhoods.

Teachers and principals are always keenly aware of the hand they have been dealt. Many understand that no public school system can supply all the people and equipment for an optimal school, and most do the best they can with the cards they have. However, the belief that the deck has been rigged so that "our" school got lost in the shuffle while others drew a full house has a profound effect on motivation. When the worst-funded schools are, almost invariably, those in the poorest areas, struggling with the most oppressive social problems, how can staff be asked to take seriously more rigorous standards and expectations?

A system that creates palpable inequalities among its schools fosters cynicism and diffuses responsibility. Some schools obviously have first pick at the best teachers, handsome new equipment and up-to-date texts, and sound, well-maintained facilities. Others are forced to make do with the teachers left over after the "bumping" process has run its course, to improvise around used textbooks and patched-up equipment, and to make sure that aging facilities are not, at the very least, hazards for the children in them. Slogans such as "All children can learn" and "High expectations for all" have a hollow ring under these circumstances.

Even fair allocation decisions can diffuse responsibility, if made secretly or in ways that signal concern with goals other than educational effectiveness. The fact that the most important assets of the school system, teachers, are allocated to preserve individuals' seniority rights rather than to maximize school effectiveness is counterproductive whether or not it creates inequalities. The belief, widespread among school staff members, that staff development time, new equipment, and maintenance and facilities renovations—not to mention the assignment of promising new teachers—are allocated according to mysterious processes, including the "pull" of individual principals and neighborhood groups, often reinforces cynicism and passivity.

When a school system's resource allocation process is not transparently fair, it encourages virtually all teachers and principals—even those who may in fact be getting more than their share—to suspect they have been somehow deprived. With that suspicion as a base, the next step is easy: Failure is not my responsibility.

Rules Instability

Uncertain resource levels are not the only cause of turbulence in the work of schools. Schools are also subject to constant changes in the rules under which they operate and the priorities advanced by the board, superintendent, and central office.

Rules instability has three sources: the shifting balance of political forces at the state and local school levels; the fragmentation of administrative responsibilities and authorities in the central office; and the constant effort to improve the schools via new programs initiated by the superintendent and board.

Schools operate as agencies of the local board, which is in turn a creature of the state government. At the state level, there is nothing to prevent uncoordinated policymaking and piecemeal legislation. New policy initiatives come from many sources, and it is up to schools to find a way to cope with them. At the local level, board members are responsible for approving budgets, hiring superintendents, approving union contracts and personnel policies, and assessing school performance. Individual board members are also responsible for representing the constituents who elected them, both in making general policy and in listening to requests and resolving disputes. The board and its individual members can have great influence over all these matters, but in practice most emphasize one of their powers, the enactment of policies that affect all schools.

Whether they are elected or appointed, board members seek office in order to improve the schools. And they do that, according to their own individual lights, by making policy. Scandals, constituent complaints, and disappointing test scores all put pressure on the board: they must do something. In most cases, that "something" constitutes enacting a policy that constrains all schools. Though some school board meetings focus on important issues, some amount of time is regularly given to the small annoyances that vex any organization: a student hit by a car while away from school grounds at lunchtime, a dispute over whether a faculty member kept proper accounts of the proceeds from a school fundraiser, a charge that a student was improperly suspended from school due to misbehavior, and so forth.

Because these small matters get dealt with by the most authoritative body in the school system, the resolution of them affects all schools. If the resolution of an issue is encoded into district policy, all schools must take immediate account of it. Even if the resolution affects only one school, personnel in other schools know that they can be sharply criticized if a similar incident occurs in their school and they have not taken account of the board's precedent. The result is that all schools must be attentive to board actions, and over time the number of board policies and precedents that schools must observe becomes very great. In Dade County, Florida, 25 schools were identified for a "site-based management pilot," which exempted them from many existing district regulations but not from future ones. But after three years, the principals in the 25 schools reported that board actions taken since the pilot began had severely eroded the freedoms they were originally promised.

The fragmentation of central administrative arrangements also creates a complex and shifting set of requirements. School district central offices are traditionally organized into many specialized units, each responsible for some aspect of school operations—management of federal and state grant programs; improvement of curriculum in some particular area, e.g., science or English; selection and upgrading of school personnel; allocation of supplies and repairs; evaluation of overall school performance; and so forth. Each of these units has its own staff and funding line; though the superintendent of schools is nominally superior to the heads of central office bureaus, his or her influence is limited. Most superintendents pick their shots carefully in trying to influence the central office. The result of central office fragmentation is that bureaus operate independently of one another, and seldom coordinate the demands they make on the schools. Though a change in school staffing or in teacher training or evaluation methods may affect all aspects of a school's program, those implications are seldom anticipated or worked through at the central office. Changes are left to be reconciled at the school level. As many principals and teachers report, the result is that they spend a great deal of time deciding how to reconcile central office directives and calculating the risks of noncompliance.

In addition to these structural sources of instability, the school reform process itself is a source of great turbulence. As Elmore and McLaughlin (1988) note, school reform has proven to be steady work:

no one has found a single-factor solution to all the schools' problems, and many bold reform strategies dissolve into tinkering at the margins. Discontent with school performance has produced constant pressure for reform. But instability of board coalitions and superintendents' tenure have led, in many big-city school systems, to successions of incompatible reforms. Top-down reforms in teacher training, testing, and curriculum have been succeeded by decentralization initiatives, followed again by efforts to tighten fiscal controls, standardize curriculum, and strengthen accountability based on student test scores. Further, as recent studies of reform processes in several big cities have shown, no reform gets enough time or money to work out. New initiatives are announced, put into place in several schools, then made subject to budget cuts, and finally succeeded by other reforms—which begin the same cycle. As shown by the Public Agenda Foundation report cited above, and by unpublished Education Commission of the States studies led by Judith Bray, the succession of conflicting initiatives has made school staffs cynical about the motives and competence of their superiors, and tentative in the implementation of any particular reform.

PRESSURES FOR PERFORMANCE

Since the mid-1960s, federal and state school policy has been preoccupied with creating pressures for improvement. In the mid-1960s it was assumed that schools were fundamentally effective institutions for most students, but that they neglected low-income, minority, and handicapped students. The reform movement of the 1980s altered the focus by charging that schools were not up to the mark in general. In the last decade, policy debate has focused on improving schools for everyone, not only the disadvantaged.

The sheer number of separate initiatives created to increase the pressure for high performance demonstrates just how difficult achieving the goal really is. Some initiatives require schools to open themselves up to advice from parents and community leaders, in the hope that greater awareness of community needs will lead to greater concern with flexibility and quality. Others have mandated more homework, more rigorous course content, and more courses in traditional subjects such as English, science, and mathematics, in the belief that too many students have avoided "solid" courses in favor of a hodgepodge of electives and applied fields such as business math and cosmetology. Still others have created statewide tests to expose school deficiencies, on the grounds that what is measured and publicized will be improved. Despite examples of some schools responding positively, in general these efforts have been demonstrable failures.

Assuring Quality

Few state or local education systems worry about quality in terms of the competence of their graduates; most systems try to assure quality by controlling inputs. They select books and curriculum materials, and they hire teachers centrally to ensure that all new recruits have degrees from accredited institutions and are eligible for state certification. Central office units also design programs of staff development to ensure that teachers are aware of new techniques. Some try to upgrade their whole teaching forces by introducing everyone to promising new concepts like cooperative learning, or by training all teachers to use a new set of textbooks or curriculum materials. The larger systems maintain specialized central office units for staff development by curriculum area. These units also provide school specialists with refresher courses and introductions to new approaches.

Despite all this activity, school systems' training and technical assistance capabilities are small. None has a budget as large as 1 percent of the entire operating budget. Business leaders, by contrast, report spending 3–4 percent of operating funds on training. Training school staffs is also expensive: substitute teachers must be paid when teachers are pulled out of the classroom for training, and union contracts require stipends for weekend or summer training. Even the most efficiently run training or staff development program is unable to assist more than a small fraction of a large district's schools in a year. Control of improvement assets is also fragmented. Though most districts have staff development directors who employ trainers and consultants, each federal or state categorical program has its own staff development budget, which is administered separately.

As noted earlier, in many school systems, the best-funded teacher training activity is controlled unilaterally by individual teachers. Teachers who attend graduate classes leading to higher degrees receive automatic wage-step increases with each small increment of graduate credit. Teachers, not principals or department heads, decide what they will study. Teachers pay their own tuition, but their wage-step increases usually reimburse all their expenses within a year. Because the step increases are permanent and become part of the base salary determining the size of future percentage wage increases, the value of the raise, over the years, is typically many times the cost of tuition. A recent study of Chicago public school expenditures (Booz-Allen & Hamilton 1992) estimated that the annual cost of such training-related wage increases was several times the district's staff development budget.

All systems gather and analyze measures of school output, e.g., student test scores and the rates of dropout, graduation, and credit completion. Aside from annual publication of such measures, few school systems have management processes intended to target trouble spots and produce improvements. Principals in many cities consistently reported that the central office rarely intervenes just because a school's performance data are poor. According to the principals, a school without financial irregularities, civil rights complaints, or incidents involving violence or racial tension is unlikely to be considered a problem for top management, even if its performance is low.

State-run quality assurance processes also focus primarily on inputs. High schools in many states must be accredited periodically, but accreditation reviews typically focus on school facilities and staffing. New York and New Jersey are exceptions to the general rule; in both, schools with consistently low student performance measures can be closed by the state. Though few schools have been closed, the possibility has led local districts, especially New York City (which contains virtually all the schools at risk of closing), to make staff changes and add new programs to some schools.

Improving Schools

The identification of "troubled" schools is often done by the press and by business groups, rather than by the school system itself. As one former superintendent said, "Once there is adverse publicity about a school, the board and superintendent have to do something about it." In most instances, however, the remedies respect existing arrangements. A "troubled" school is likely to get new equipment and additional staff to run new programs. But these resources are typically added on top of what is already in place, and they have few, if any, consequences for the staff in the school. As the Cincinnati Youth Collaborative found in trying to turn around troubled Taft High School, the system will accept additions to a school but can do little to change its basic operations.

This incremental approach to quality improvement has many causes, including the division of the central office into independent specialist divisions, civil service employment protection for teachers and administrators, and inflexible rules governing the use of state and federal categorical program funds. But the most important limitation on quality improvement is the school systems' lack of uncommitted funds to invest in problem solving. Due to the politically competitive nature of school system budgetmaking, virtually all funds are captured by existing commitments, especially employment contracts with teachers.

A very small number of school systems have created staff development/technical assistance centers dedicated to helping schools make more fundamental improvements. These centers—which often depend on funds from local businesses or foundations rather than the school system itself—exist to respond to schools' requests. The best-developed model is the Gheens Academy in Louisville, which tailor-makes staff training programs to the needs of individual schools at the initiative of either the school or the central office. Services can range from short-term classes and workshops to connecting the school with an organization that specializes in the transformation of whole schools, such as the Coalition of Essential Schools. The Mayerson Academy, a business-funded center in Cincinnati, is now providing a similar mix of services. Teacher unions in New York, Miami, Chicago, and Los Angeles are gearing up to create similar centers; their capacities, however, will be small relative to the size of the school system.

In the late 1980s, a foundation-funded center in Pittsburgh, Schenley, trained entire school staffs in new curricula and teaching techniques. When a staff was scheduled for the Schenley Center, the school system would send in a whole new staff to run the school. Teachers and administrators attended classes together at Schenley for two weeks, practiced new methods in an experimental school located at the center, and observed and critiqued each other. Schenley depended on major donations from businesses and foundations, and it closed in the early 1990s.

Such arrangements for school-specific assistance are rare. In most school systems, staff development programs reflect the tastes and agendas of central office staff and categorical program coordinators and do not directly support school initiative.

Student Protection

Though several states guarantee every student (in the words of the New Jersey constitution) "a thorough and efficient education," public school systems are designed to manage institutions, not to ensure individual benefits. Only handicapped children are guaranteed an education that is appropriate to their needs (under P.L. 94-142, the Education for All Handicapped Children Act). If a neighborhood school does not provide what a handicapped child needs, the parents can demand that it create a new program or transfer the child to another school.

But about 90 percent of all children are not covered by P.L. 94-142. For these youngsters, no mechanism exists to ensure they get exactly what they need. Parents can obtain action if they demonstrate that their child's school has been starved of resources, and they can petition for a transfer to another school. The school system, however, enjoys great discretion in responding to such petitions, and parents must be prepared to devote a great deal of time and energy pursuing them. For all practical purposes, the public school system is not designed to ensure that the individual student gets what he or she needs.

Public school systems do accept a responsibility for meeting the distinctive needs of groups of students. This responsibility, based more on educators' personal values and customary practices than on any enforceable legal rights, can lead public school systems to do heroic things. For example, the Miami public schools' response to waves of Cuban and Haitian refugees, and their basic commitment to educating immigrant students—whoever they are and whatever they need—is remarkable. The same could be said for many California school systems serving refugees and immigrants.

In every school district with more than a few schools, however, teachers and administrators whisper in private about the performance of some schools and the personnel within them. Day in and day out, year in and year out, and, by now it is not too much to say, decade in and decade out, some schools have consistently failed to educate the vast majority of the students enrolled in them. No governance system can ensure that every adult employed to teach children will be either competent *or* caring, much less competent *and* caring; on occasion, teachers and administrators may be neither. In any human organization, performance varies and unpredictable problems crop up. Successful organizations identify problems quickly and respond effectively. Schools, as discussed above, rarely do either.

Yet the obligation of school systems to both identify and solve problems is particularly high, because the people who most directly observe their performance, children, are not qualified to judge quality. Moreover, the individuals who receive the service, again children, have no choice but to do so.

The fact remains that some groups of students are highly likely to fail in today's public schools. African American students are as likely to drop out of high school as to finish, and those who do finish school and take the Scholastic Assessment Test (formerly Scholastic Aptitude Test) are likely to score below the 25th percentile for white students. Much the same is true for the U.S.-born children of Hispanic immigrants. As Kozol (1992) and the plaintiffs in *Rodriguez* v. *Anton* have demonstrated, the public school system delivers less to them— less money, more dilapidated school buildings, fewer and poorer-prepared teachers, and fewer books—than to other students.

No one with any first-hand knowledge of how schools serving these youngsters operate, or with direct responsibility for their quality, has *ever* argued that these schools are adequate. When challenged about the adequacy of the services provided in such schools, administrators invariably fall back on the defense of process, procedures, and compliance with applicable rules and regulations. They make no claim that the system is structured to ensure that these students succeed in school. There is every good reason for not making such an argument: the claim cannot survive even cursory examination. As courts have recently decided in Kentucky, Alabama, and West Virginia, the current arrangements for providing public education do not deliver what students need and deserve.

Opportunity is distributed in public schools just as it is in the economy: everybody has some chance to succeed. The practical effect of this opportunity, in school as in the free market, is that some people have a much better chance than others. Today's public schools are not required to do whatever is necessary to make a particular student succeed. Many educators will consider the idea that schools have responsibilities beyond delivering instruction, indeed an obligation to make sure every student succeeds, to be an unfair imposition on them.

Compulsory schooling is the gentlest and most benign of the many ways that government limits individual freedom in democratic societies. Schooling is not simply a public service provided in the hope that citizens will enjoy it or feel good about its availability; in virtually every state and local jurisdiction, it is the law of the land that parents enroll their children up to the age of fifteen or sixteen. Children are required, that is to say forced, to go to school. They are forced to do so because the community has an overriding interest in ensuring that each child is educated well enough to participate fully in adult economic and political life. Since schools deprive people of their freedom, they assume a very heavy burden: they must ensure that *every* child in fact receives the benefits held out as a justification for the loss of freedom. That obligation means that a school system's claim that it made a reasonable effort with a particular child is not good enough. It is not enough to show that the form of schooling provided in a particular school works more often than it fails. If the regulations and civil service rules developed to organize the working relationships of the adults lead to ineffective schools, they must be changed. A government agency that deprives students of their freedom must make a serious effort to educate every child, without exception.

The bureaucratic character of public education ensures that schools do a reasonably good job of protecting students from certain kinds of failures. Despite the publicity they receive, sexual abuse, blatant, overt racial discrimination, and physical abuse of children are relatively rare. When any of these abuses appear, they are *always* treated as emergencies; the system generally responds quickly, often by suspending staff pending investigations, substituting new staff, and adding training, counseling, and other programs to guarantee safe custody of the minors in their care. Unfortunately, the system is much less surefooted in dealing with chronic, long-term problems, e.g., health hazards, deteriorating buildings, poor relationships with parents and the community, and academic failure. The system's basic decisionmaking structure, with its emphasis on keeping peace among adults and protecting job rights—makes it hard to close, replace, or fundamentally alter schools that fail children.

As long as school boards, superintendents, and central offices concentrate on protecting the entire system and its institutions from as much disturbance as possible, in part by permitting marginal improvements here and there, public schools will not change. A good governance system for public education would attach far greater importance to intervention on behalf of children whose schools have failed them. It would display the same passion for achievement that most systems already demonstrate for student safety. It would attack school failure just as it now attacks school violence.

CONCLUSIONS

The system sketched in this chapter is not aesthetically pleasing. Rule-bound, it discourages initiative and risk taking in schools and systems facing unprecedented problems. Politically driven, it allows decisions reached from on high that satisfy as many people as possible to substitute for the professional judgment and initiative of competent, caring professionals in the school and classroom. Emphasizing compliance, it defines accountability as adherence to process, when results are the only appropriate standard. Organized to manage institutions and minimize conflict, it ties up resources on permanent staff and the management of routine operations.

Under the current system, schools have no incentive to make pledges about what students will experience or attain or to critique their own performance. When schools succeed they are seldom reproduced, and when they fail they are seldom closed or restaffed. Few staff members benefit greatly from working in an excellent school or suffer much from working in a mediocre one.

Despite the critical nature of the analysis in this chapter, however, we should remember that the current system has a major advantage over many alternatives: it exists. It collects and spends public funds, manages schools, and processes students through them with minimal interruptions or uncertainties. It may not use funds efficiently or produce high-quality results for all students, but it does operate. In contrast, the alternatives defined in subsequent chapters do not exist on a large scale anywhere in the United States, and their capacity to provide stable and reliable school operations for thousands of students remains to be demonstrated.

Chapter Four

CONTRACTING

In the course of this project the study team considered and discarded many possible alternative systems of governance. Although there are apparently promising models in business, public service, and foreign and private educational systems, none fits U.S. public education well. Even the public education systems in other English-speaking countries were hard to adapt because they were, relative to the U.S. systems, more likely to accept unequal outcomes for different groups and less concerned about separation of church and state. The models of governance that the research team ultimately considered were domestic in origin. We examined how large multisite law firms encourage performance and maintain the quality of the services they deliver from site to site. We looked into how the U.S. Department of State tries to ensure consistently high-quality work in its diverse operations around the globe. We focused intently on recent governance experiments and proposals in American education itself.

Despite their differences in mission, approach, and goals, what all of these models hold in common can be reduced to several characteristics that can help define an alternative governance system for schools. These characteristics include the following:

- **Self-reliance**. In successful enterprises, dispersed service delivery organizations are encouraged to be as self-reliant and enterprising as possible.

- **Local control**. Local units are offered as much control as possible over critical factors (money and staff) of production and service.

- **Flexibility.** Inflexible arrangements with key suppliers or with civil service personnel systems, which make it difficult for unsuccessful local organizations to be changed or eliminated, are avoided.

- **Local accountability.** Accounting for results is based on specific goals of local units and the needs of local clients, not on general rules.

- **Assistance in place of direction.** Top corporate managers and central staff emphasize providing resources to help local units succeed, intervening only to avert disasters.

- **Problem solving.** At the local level, policy favors problem solving, not control.

The model presented in this chapter is drawn from many sources. Ted Kolderie's work on charter schools shows how independently run public schools can exist as exceptions within the current governance system. Charter schools (see Kolderie 1992; Nathan 1989) permit groups to run publicly funded schools under explicit contracts with the local school board. Chubb and Moe's (1990) proposal for market systems provided useful insights into the value of greater choice in school selection, for both parents and teachers. Osborne and Gaebler's (1992) ideas about improving the quality of public services by encouraging competition between public agencies and private contractors offered important lessons. RAND researcher Michael Mack's analysis of the experience of Education Alternatives, Inc., a private firm with contracts to operate public schools in Baltimore, Miami, St. Paul, and Phoenix, convinced us that local public authorities can dramatically change their style of operation.

WHAT SCHOOL CONTRACTING MEANS

The thesis of this report is that the key to a new governance system for public education is contracting. Public school systems can have all the characteristics listed above if every school is a separate entity, capable of entering into legally enforceable contracts with public officials responsible for education. Schools operating under contract would control their own budgets, hire and evaluate their own staff, attract students on the basis of clear promises about what will be provided, and survive or fail on their ability to meet goals individually negotiated in light of the school's goals and the needs of its clientele.

Contracting would preserve public education by reinventing it. Unlike the current system, in which all public schools are both funded and operated by government bureaucracies, contracting emphasizes the establishment of schools operated by a variety of public and private organizations under the oversight of a public body.

Under contracting, schools would be run by independent organizations under contract with state or local public education agencies. Schools would be independent enterprises, operating under applicable state laws and local rules and explicit contract terms specifying what kind of instruction was to be delivered, to whom and by whom, and with what results. As in a market system, students and teachers would choose and be chosen by schools; no one would have an automatic right to administer, teach in, or attend a particular school.

Contract schools could use existing public school buildings and equipment, thus avoiding major upfront investments while they build a reputation and clientele. Contractors would be guaranteed a minimum level of income for the duration of the contract. Contracts would, however, specify that schools failing to attract a minimum level of enrollment, or failing to produce specified student outcomes, could be closed and their funding terminated.

Local school boards might exist, as at present, or the state might create new local or regional entities in their place. States or local agencies would not run schools; they would contract for them with independent organizations. Some of these independent organizations could be the staffs and parents of existing successful schools, for example, neighborhood schools with good records of serving their students and communities or magnet schools with well-defined programs and histories of success with average, as well as exceptional, students. Other school contracts could be established through the issuance of public requests for proposals, and still others might be negotiated directly with community groups or educational institutions that offer to run one or more schools.

State governments could create performance standards that would apply to all contract schools. Like existing state licensing and student graduation requirements for private schools, these standards could limit the range of possible schooling approaches, but they should not be so specific as to force all schools to be alike. Each school's contract would specify the school's mission, instructional emphasis, admissions practices, and student outcome expectations. Contracts would run for specific periods and be automatically renewed if all aspects of performance were satisfactory. Contractors whose performance was mediocre could be forced to compete for renewals with rivals in the world of educational services.

As presented in greater detail below, contracting is an alternative form of governance for an entire school system. It is based on the proposition that public schools are most likely to become effective if they are freed from micromanagement by political bodies. Public schools run under contract can be focused, either on the effective delivery of a particular mode of instruction for those who want it or on flexible problem solving on behalf of a defined group of students. In such schools, teachers and principals can assume responsibility for what they produce, and parents can hold them accountable, both for delivering the promised instruction and school climate and for getting results. Such schools give teachers and principals strong incentives to collaborate, to press one another for good performance rather than to tolerate or work around incompetence, and to work as hard as necessary to serve their students. Under contracting, all public schools, not just a select few, could have these characteristics.

Public school contracting is based on a simple insight about effective schools, namely, that virtually all of them have something that sets them apart: a warrant to be focused and distinctive, to do something in particular well rather than to go through the motions of being all things to all people. The warrant to be focused and distinctive might be based on the local school board's need to provide a school for a defined group or to provide skills demanded by an industry or a sector of higher education. The warrant might also be based on a good idea: an innovative way of motivating ordinary students, using technology, or marshaling the efforts of teachers. The warrant might, perhaps most importantly, be based on the staff's demonstrated intention to provide rigorous and effective instruction by disciplined use of conventional methods. Whatever its origin, the contract school's warrant supersedes many of the rules and operating procedures that now govern school systems.

Under the current governance system, a small number of schools, mostly magnets and recipients of foundation grants, have such warrants. Some schools' warrants are written and explicit, and some are based only on tacit agreements with the school system's central office. But in every case a school's warrant for being focused and distinctive is essentially a contract, specifying what mission the school will pursue, whom it will serve and how, and on what grounds the school's special status will be continued. The governance system sketched in this section applies this insight to public school governance generally.

The system described below could work in the vast majority of U.S. school systems. Any system that has multiple schools can hold multiple contracts, one for each school. Even small-town and rural school systems with only one large school could create two or more smaller schools within the same building and thereby benefit from the flexibility, diversity, and performance pressures that contracting provides. The only kind of school system in which contracting would not make a difference is one in which existing schools are geographically isolated and too small to subdivide. Many such schools now operate as virtually independent corporations, and formal contracting might stabilize their independent status but would not change it fundamentally.

DEFINITION OF A PUBLIC SCHOOL

Under a contracting scheme, a public school would be one run under contract with a local public education authority. School boards would own public schools and finance public education, but they would not staff or operate buildings. The contractor could be a public agency—including ad hoc organizations created by parents and staff of existing schools—or any of a wide variety of private nonprofit and profit-making organizations. But local public school boards would not run schools themselves or create public bureaucracies to do so.

Any organization, profit-making or nonprofit, would be eligible to enter into a contract to manage one or more schools. Public education authorities could set minimum qualifications for potential contractors, but these would be broad enough to allow noneducators to offer to develop and manage schools. Contractors could include universities, civic groups, businesses, church groups willing to admit all students and run completely nonsectarian schools, teacher cooperatives, teacher unions, and other organizations put together expressly to serve a particular group of students or use a particular instructional method.

Kolderie (1992) has identified several alternative providers of public contract schools:

- One local district could offer a school in the territory of another. A city could set up an alternative school for at-risk children in the suburbs.

- Colleges and universities could be encouraged to reopen the K–12 schools they once ran.

- Two or more local units of general government, taking advantage of state "joint powers" laws, might combine to do together what neither is allowed to do alone—e.g., the local education agency (LEA) might work with local health or housing authorities to provide them with the authority to run a school.

- The state itself could create schools directly, as some have for the arts and math and science. Or the state board of education could seek authority to sponsor new schools or set up an agency to do so.

- The federal government might establish some model schools on the TVA principle, as a "yardstick" for local performance, instead of writing checks to states and superintendents.

In addition to these public agencies, a wide range of private social service, educational, and entrepreneurial organizations, such as Education Alternatives, Inc. and Whittle Communications' Edison Schools, could also enter contracts to provide schools.

Contractors would use public school buildings at no cost, and the local public education authority would provide a negotiated amount for utilities, incidental repairs, and maintenance; capital expenditures not specific to the contractor's instructional methods would be made by the public education authority.

FUNDING

Public funds for schools would continue to be raised from a combination of local and state taxes and federal grants. The local public authority would pay contractors by combining funds from all sources. Contractors would have to account for their overall use of funds, but they would not have to segment their accounting or service delivery to demonstrate compliance with categorical program requirements. Contracts would, in the vast majority of cases, be based on a standard local per-pupil amount. Local public agencies would be free, however, to negotiate a slightly higher than average per-pupil rate for schools in the lowest income areas, where children often need additional support and smaller classes are often essential.

Schools' total funding would be based on estimated enrollment and would be adjusted in light of experience. To stabilize school services, contractors would start each school year with a guaranteed minimum amount of funds, which would be increased immediately if enrollment exceeded expectations. In schools whose enrollment was equal to or higher than expected, total funding would be precisely equal to the average per-pupil expenditure (less a small amount retained to cover the school system's contract administration costs) times the number of students enrolled. After a year in which enrollment fell below expectations, contracts would provide for a reduction in assured minimum funding for a school. If a school's enrollment fell below the minimum set by contract, either party (the contractor or LEA) would be free to terminate it.

Contracting could allow for, but not automatically accommodate, differential funding for students from different demographic and income groups. Absolute equality in local per-pupil funding would be a major benefit for disadvantaged groups. Since 1965, federal and state governments have provided "categorical" grants to pay for extra services to low-income, handicapped, and language-minority children. These can add as much as 20 percent to a school's funding.

However, as several recent studies and lawsuits have shown, schools that get most of the categorical grant money are frequently shortchanged in the distribution of other resources, and categorical grant funds are too small to equalize funding. So despite a declared policy of providing extra resources to the neediest schools, most localities in fact give them much less. By bringing all schools up to true equality of funding, contracting can dramatically, and promptly, increase funding for schools in the most troubled inner-city areas. The first contracts negotiated for such areas would be based on the districtwide average per-pupil expenditure.

ORGANIZING LEARNING

The core purpose of contracting is to create schools with clear, simple missions and definite strategies for motivating students and delivering instruction. Contracts would, therefore, be expected to cover the goals and methods that particular schools will use. These goals and methods could be formulated by the potential contractors themselves. In Baltimore, for example, Education Alternatives, Inc. proposed, and gained a school board contract to provide, eight schools based on extensive use of computer-paced instruction. Goals and methods could also be formulated by a local public education agency seeking to provide a school that meets a defined need (e.g., a school emphasizing apprenticeship-style education) or to meet an organized demand (e.g., a school with high academic standards emphasizing African culture and history).

However formulated, a school's mission and approach would be written into the contract. The specification of these elements, along with the basic state licensing and graduation requirements that now apply to all private schools, would become the foundation for public control over the school's curriculum and pedagogy and, ultimately, the judgments about the school's performance.

State or local school boards could require that all contractors cover the state-mandated curriculum and that all students pass certain exams (e.g., statewide student proficiency tests). They could not, however, specify curriculum so tightly that contractors were forced into the box confining today's public schools, i.e., essentially required to run identical instructional programs.

SCHOOL STAFFING AND TEACHER CAREERS

If public schools were run under contract, the terms of employment for many teachers would change dramatically. Schools, or the contractors that run them, would employ teachers. Because they were responsible for their own budgets and staffing patterns, schools could employ different mixes of junior and senior teachers and un-certified subject matter specialists, determine their own stu-dent/teacher ratios, and set their own pay scales. Individual teachers might own some schools, and others might be run as partnerships among several teachers. Teachers who became "the heart and soul" of a school could make more money and enjoy more professional opportunities than current civil service structures allow. Teachers would become, as many have long wanted to be, independent pro-fessionals able to guide their own careers and benefit from special-ized knowledge or good personal reputations.

School contractors would hire teachers, either on the open market or from a registry of certified teachers, depending on the terms of the contract. The local education authority could set minimum teacher pay scales, and state and federal specifications of employment con-ditions (e.g., wage, health, and safety laws) would apply. Apart from that regulatory framework, decisions about hiring, promotion, and assignment of individuals would be made by the school or the con-tractor responsible for it.

The contract system would lead to the creation of a labor market for instructional and administrative staff. As independent enterprises, schools would choose, evaluate, and terminate their own staff mem-bers, and staff would be free to select, assess, and make their own choices about where to teach. Teacher salary scales might be set by the market, so that teachers could gain higher pay in recognition of sterling personal reputations, or to compensate for working in espe-cially difficult situations or carrying especially heavy responsibilities. Some might also accept lower pay in order to work in highly attrac-tive schools. A given school might decide to hire a relatively small number of experienced, highly paid teachers, or it might opt for a larger number of cheaper, less experienced teachers. But most schools would, like private schools, live within their budgets by em-ploying a mix of staff members, ranging from the few highly experi-enced "mainstays" to the more numerous new college graduates, who may have more current or advanced training on subject matter but lack classroom experience. No school could afford to have a large staff composed entirely of highly paid senior teachers (as is now the case in many city schools), and few schools could survive if they relied entirely on low-cost, inexperienced teachers (as is also the case in many public schools in low-income urban areas).

As Ted Kolderie has suggested, many schools might be run by teacher cooperatives or by existing teacher unions. In such cases, teachers would be like partners in a law or architecture firm, able to establish positive professional working conditions but also responsible for the kind of frank mutual assessment that leads to a healthy and competitive organization. Teachers would also be as mobile as other professionals, able to accept better opportunities offered by schools other than their present employer, and required to look for the school where their own skills and work habits are most appreciated. As in any such labor market, teachers who could make themselves attractive to many schools would be better paid and more securely employed than teachers who did not establish positive personal reputations.

As Coons and Sugarman (1978) show, many teachers will find their lives far more rewarding if they can work in schools where initiative is regarded and performance counts. Less senior teachers are also likely to find that their choices of schools are improved, as well as their opportunities for making better salaries in return for excellent work. Many productive senior teachers will also appreciate the better working environments in schools that must win good reputations and maintain high levels of performance.

STUDENT ASSIGNMENT

Each school's processes and standards for student selection would be set by its contract. A generally applicable requirement would prohibit discriminatory practices by insisting on random selection from the list of all who apply. No contractor would be allowed to handpick students or set admission standards unrelated to the school's mission. Thus, for example, a performing arts school might require auditions, and a school focused on higher mathematics could require prerequisite courses; but schools could not set admissions requirements based on measures of general academic ability. Schools would remain, despite their varied missions and structures, public schools serving public ends.

Though virtually any student could gain admission to any school, the school would be free to impose requirements for student effort and progress, as long as those requirements were explicit, understood from the very first day, and fairly applied. Schools would also be obligated to publish their methods for helping students having academic difficulty. Students who would not do the required work or could not make academic progress despite receiving all the help the school promised could be counseled to leave the school. State or local public authorities could require, however, that a consistent pattern of failure among disadvantaged or minority students would lead to a review of the school's contract.

Despite the fact that students would be free to apply to any school, the local education authority would have to be vigilant about the educational opportunities available to low-income and minority students, especially those living in troubled inner-city neighborhoods. Parents in those areas might find it especially difficult to transport their children elsewhere, and local residents and merchants might want to keep a school to anchor the community. In such cases, local school boards might want to attract contractors otherwise reluctant to operate in difficult environments, requiring them to give neighborhood children first preference in admissions.

If local education authorities found it difficult to hire contractors willing to operate in inner-city areas or serve a clientele made up largely of disadvantaged youngsters, they could offer inducements in the form of higher than average per-pupil payments. Organizations operating more than one school in a district might also be required to run a specified number of schools in low-income or otherwise troubled areas, a guarantee that the most capable contractors could not evade the toughest problems. (In Baltimore, Education Alternatives, Inc. was induced to take responsibility for a troubled junior high school as a condition of its contract to run eight elementary schools.) Such a requirement also creates the conditions under which all contractors must develop competence to educate students with many problems. In addition, since contractors have no desire to be responsible for a school with a bad reputation, most would take steps to insure that none of their schools, even in the most difficult neighborhoods, was considered a "dumping ground" for troublesome students and staff.

A contract school system, like any other, would have to take account of the inevitability that some students would not meet any normal school's attendance and effort requirements.   Contract schools would have the strongest possible incentive to help students having difficulty, to keep enrollments up and avoid suspicion that they had not offered enough help to students who could have succeeded. But contract schools must ultimately be free to conclude that they cannot help a student, the student will not help herself, or the student's continued enrollment will destroy the school's credibility with other students and parents.   For such cases, a contract school system might need to include "alternative schools," specially designed to motivate and help such students.   Most school systems of any size now have such schools, and many already work under special arrangements that resemble contracts.   Some school systems, in fact, contract out for the alternative schools with organizations like Ombudsman of Libertyville, Illinois.   Ombudsman runs contract alternative schools for several communities in the Midwest and Southwest for amounts no greater than the districtwide per-pupil expenditure.   Its rates of student attendance, graduation, and subsequent college and job placement are much higher than those for comparable students in regular schools.

ENCOURAGING INITIATIVE

At its heart, contracting is designed to make schools independent and competitive enterprises. By definition, on this criterion it is far superior to the present system, because existing governance systems are designed to make schools clones of each other, dependent on central offices for resources, and accountable largely for compliance with rules imposed from outside and above.

The educational essence of contracting is that it requires local public education agencies to make educational decisions on a school-by-school basis. This requirement represents a major change from today's practice. Today, regardless of the nature, severity, or duration of a school's aches and pains, school board physicians prescribe a single treatment. Most schools remain healthy if they keep an eye on their diet and exercise regularly. Others require a band-aid to encourage small abrasions to heal. Some need major surgery. The governance system treats every ailment as a fever. Aspirin is the treatment of choice, since it keeps community temperatures down, and all schools are required to take it.

Contracting changes all that. Under contracting, the school board need not ask whether a school concept is right for all the students in the district, or whether some stakeholder groups would dislike a particular school. All the board need ask is whether there is a demand for a particular kind of program, whether there is reason to think the proposed academic program can be effective if it is well delivered, whether the people proposing to run the school have plausible credentials for doing so, and whether the options available districtwide satisfy the full range of demands and needs in the district.

Under contracting, a school must attract students if it is to survive over the long haul. The pressures on schools to offer something that makes them stand out—a distinctive curriculum, social climate, or extracurricular program—will be significant. Only by distinguishing themselves from run-of-the-mill offerings can schools hope to attract the interest of potential students and their parents, a prerequisite for persuading them to enroll.

Schools must deliver on their promises if their reputations are to survive. In addition to maintaining a distinctive and consistent program, a school must develop a reputation for quality, such that parents expect their children's opportunities for employment and higher education to be increased, not compromised. They must deliver on their promises well enough to keep current students from transferring out, create "brand loyalty" among families with several children, and attract enough new families to fill the entering class each year.

That is a demanding set of requirements. Some of today's public schools might feel intimidated by them, but they are far from unheard-of outside the protected enclave of public schooling. Private colleges and universities meet those criteria every year. Private elementary and secondary schools of all descriptions—inner-city parochial and bucolic preparatory schools—meet the challenge of establishing an identity, building a reputation for quality, and maintaining consumer loyalty. Even religious schools, which often benefit from parents' attachment to the sponsoring institution, can live and die on their reputations for consistency and quality. As Celio (1995) has documented, many Catholic schools that closed in the 1970s did so because their traditional clients concluded they offered little to set them apart from public schools and produced little better in the way of results. Conversely, Catholic schools that survived were those with well-grounded educational traditions and the skills to maintain quality.

The need to build identity and reputation encourages a number of school staff behaviors that "effective schools" advocates consider essential. School staff must articulate a mission for the school and work hard to make sure all elements of the school contribute to attaining school goals. Under contracting, administrators and teachers have strong incentives to do just that. The mission should be easy to communicate and meaningful to parents; it should focus on what children will experience in school and what they will be able to do on leaving it, not on subtleties of educational technique comprehensible only to professionals. Contracting puts a premium on meaningful communication with parents and prospective parents.

Effective schools advocates believe teachers need to work in teams and to be concerned about the overall effectiveness of the school. A mission stated in terms of the desired attributes of students leaving the school helps teachers understand how their particular class or subject matter contributes to the school's final product. As studies of "special" public schools have shown, this focus on mission makes teachers understand how they depend on one another and encourages efforts to identify the school's deficiencies and help remedy them. (See Lipsitz 1983; Hill, Foster, and Gendler 1990.)

The demands of sheer economic survival also encourage teachers to be concerned about the performance of the school as a whole and about the contributions of their peers. In a contracting system, when a school is forced to close because too few students want to attend or the district decides performance does not meet promises, all teachers and administrators have to find new jobs, no matter how well they taught their own classes. Staff members therefore have strong incentives to help one another, identify weaknesses, and ensure that variations in teacher performance do not harm the school's ultimate product and reputation.

FAIR AND STABLE RESOURCES AND RULES

A contracting system would lead to a more equitable allocation of resources among schools than the present system. Even if it accomplishes no other purposes, it allocates funds among all contractors entirely on a per-student basis. Contracting lacks a sure solution to the problems of unequal per-pupil funding among districts within a state, or for resource instability caused by rises and falls in state revenues; but it certainly solves the within-district problem.

Public school boards operating through contracts would allocate cash, in the form of a fixed per-student reimbursement payment from the local education authority to the school. Contracting is designed to ensure that virtually all the money available for the public education system is spent in the schools. Local education agencies would still exist and could claim some money for administration. But all remaining funds would go to the schools as cash. Schools would, in effect, be free to buy whatever they needed on the market, and most services provided by current local education agencies could survive only if they attracted voluntary customers.

A major benefit of contracting is that it forces all school costs into the open. Most existing per-pupil expenditure figures are of little assistance in helping the public understand how much money is actually spent on teaching and learning activities per pupil. Existing figures are not learning expenditures at all, but the costs of running the system, with all its attendant costs for servicing debt, paying salaries and fringe benefits, running a major transportation system, and, in most cities, providing more meals than the local restaurant industry. Contracting opens up the possibility of focusing public attention on expenditures per student at the school site.

Contracting requires schools to negotiate wage and benefit packages with each individual teacher or administrator. No entity other than the school itself could pick up "hidden" costs such as those for fringe benefits and retirement. Groups of schools might hire an independent organization to provide services ranging from staff training and recruitment to benefit and retirement packages. But these services would be funded solely out of the cash payments made by the public education authority to the schools, payments based solely on the per-student allotment.

Schools would enjoy substantial freedom in how they used their money. State regulations or contract-boilerplate language could set minimum qualifications for the school principal and a few members of the instructional staff, but few such prescriptions would be warranted. In general, schools would compete on performance and would be free to configure themselves and select staff members according to a site-specific plan. Any other arrangement would make it harder to run distinctive programs, quickly returning school governance to the very problem it needs to avoid, namely, stifling standardization of structure and practice.

Contracting would create a much fairer distribution of staff among schools than the existing system allows. As explained earlier, the existing system permits unilateral placement decisions by senior teachers to determine the distribution of resources among schools. This situation, and the fact that central office services, including maintenance and repair, are typically allocated on a "squeaky wheel" basis, means that students in low-income areas often receive the benefit of far fewer real resources than students in more advantaged areas of the same school district.

There can be no more stable governance system than the current one. Its stability is at once its major strength and its greatest weakness. It survives by accommodating all of the diverse political and societal demands placed on schools. It does the best it can to mollify everyone with a demand, even at the cost of constraining schools so much that they cannot do anything well.

A contracting system could also be stable. A school with a contract would have legally enforceable rights to continue operating and receiving public money as long as it performs as promised. In contrast, schools operating under existing site-based management or magnet school schemes remain part of the school system bureaucracy and therefore vulnerable to changes in administrative or political signals. They can maintain their independence and special character only as long as a majority of the local school board supports them. Site-managed schools like Chicago's depend on waivers that can be revoked at any minute. Even the charter schools recently established under state laws in Minnesota, California, Massachusetts, and other states have no legally enforceable rights. They can last only as long as a majority of the school board is willing to tolerate them—in other words, only as long as they are not controversial.

Legally enforceable contracts let schools that are performing well survive controversy. As a system, contracting also gives public authorities a better way to handle political conflict. It assumes that conflict and diverse demands are inevitable. Its response to this, however, is not to mollify every demand everywhere, but to make sure that the system accommodates every demand somewhere. It holds the promise of protecting individual schools from the turbulence of educational politics while deflecting political pressures in a productive fashion. It does so by sidestepping the need for consensus on curriculum content and instructional methods, and consciously fostering diversity on the very issues on which Americans are most divided.

Contracting implies a commitment to diversity in educational offerings. Schools choose or are commissioned to provide particular kinds of services. Basic civil rights guarantees and employee protections would still apply, but a school would not be required to take actions incompatible with its basic mission or approach. For example, a school commissioned to provide bilingual instruction to Spanish-speaking immigrants would not be required to offer courses for Mandarin speakers, even though the school system might be obligated to create a school or program for that purpose elsewhere. A school offering a curriculum designed for African American boys might be required to admit white girls if they applied, but it would not be required to change its curriculum to accommodate them.

A community, parent, or educators' group that desired a particular form of multicultural curriculum or classes urging approval of alternative lifestyles might be able to obtain them in a particular school. Nevertheless, the same group could not hope to have the services they want mandated for the whole school system, and would have few incentives to do so. Such diversity permits each school to focus on a defined mission and to differentiate its products from other schools.

If no one approach to schooling is universally required, there is little need to resolve educational differences through political means. Different tastes and preferences can find expression in different schools. It would be possible, therefore, for individual schools or groups of schools to adopt definite approaches to schooling and to become, in effect, fully aligned and standards-driven. The success of networks of schools connected with Montessori, Waldorf, Paideia, and religious groups attests to the power of such alignment.

Diversity is an inevitable by-product of any reform based on increasing schools' independence. If schools are independent they will take on a character that reflects the needs and values of community, staff, or students, and they will appeal to students and new staff members on the basis of affinity. Contracting accentuates the pressures for diversity by forcing school staffs to explain their assumptions and approaches to public authorities and to make specific claims about what students will learn. Given the wide range of social, cultural, and language groups served by public education, public schools under a contract system will inevitably come to define different goals and pursue different approaches.

Diversity brings its own problems. Many fear that diversity might encourage public support of schools run by hate groups and cults or give rise to schools teaching dogmatic creationism or "flat-earth theories." Such problems may arise, but they may also be teapot tempests. It is not easy to run a school under even the best circumstances; fringe groups are likely to be discouraged by the problem of competing with high-quality "mainstream" alternatives.

Nonetheless, the very possibility that fringe groups might be encouraged to establish contract schools means that elected officials can face some difficult decisions: Should districts contract with groups propounding divisive ideologies or lacking any experience as educators? Local education authorities could resolve such issues by contracting only with organizations that have track records running schools, including the staffs of existing public and private schools, teacher unions and cooperatives, higher education institutions, school reform networks, and school management firms. More perplexing difficulties may arise about whether to contract for schools on the outer boundaries of traditional educational practice or content. Such decisions will inevitably involve balancing the interests of competing groups; that is, the decisions will be political.

These issues are complex, but they should not be any more difficult to resolve under contracting than under the current system. Demands of fringe groups now take up a significant part of many urban school boards' agendas. Under contracting, the fringe groups will focus their demands on whether they get authority to run a particular school, not whether their views should be incorporated in the curricula of all schools. A state or local school board can, therefore, address such issues as boundary-setting questions, not fundamental ones. Political conflict might still be harsh, but the majority of schools will be unaffected by it. Virtually all of the educational approaches traditionally permitted in licensed private schools will be eligible for operation under simple contracts. Only proponents of educational ideas representing fringe interests hostile to major groups in society are at risk of being denied the opportunity to provide schools.

PRESS FOR HIGH PERFORMANCE

Contracting would create pressures for performance in the same way that it would encourage initiative and responsibility among school staffs, through competition. The need to attract students encourages high performance. Contracting responds to a need identified in recent years by Albert Shanker, president of the American Federation of Teachers. Schools, says Shanker, are the only institutions that he knows of in which "if you do something good, nothing happens, and if you do something bad, nothing happens." Contracting is a governance system designed to both reward schools that gain reputations for quality and punish schools with bad records.

Under contracting, a school that gains a reputation for low quality is in danger of losing, first, its student enrollment and, ultimately, its public funding. The prospect of being forced to close the school is a great motivation for teachers and administrators. Because teachers and administrators are employees of the school, not of the local district, they have no automatic reinstatement rights elsewhere. On the positive side, because the local school system's central office will be reduced to a contracting agency, schools will have more money to spend. According to a number of studies of central office spending (Booz-Allen & Hamilton 1992; Cooper 1993), cutting central office spending by one-third would substantially increase funding at the school level. School-level funding is now approximately two-thirds of total per-pupil expenditure. If elimination of the large central office civil service staffs saved only half the money now spent outside the schools, spending at the school level could increase immediately by nearly 15 percent.

Schools could also use their funds more efficiently. Schools would be free to allocate their income as needed: if they need to spend less on driver's training, substitute teachers, or elective courses, and more to hire a highly qualified math teacher or to send an English teacher for retraining, they can do so. They will need permission from no one. Staff development will not be mandated from on high; schools should have the resources and freedom to buy what they need. Like private schools, schools run under contract would have responsibility for their own staff development and quality control. These services, which are now centrally administered and therefore unresponsive to individual school needs, would be purchased by schools on the open market. Though some cost savings related to the existing system are likely, contracts must include reasonable funding for staff training, self-assessment, and adoption of promising new teaching methods and technologies.

The contracting system expressly allows for new kinds of nongovernmental institutions that can help schools maintain quality. Local public education authorities will not want to execute separate contracts with dozens, or in some cities hundreds, of individual schools. They will prefer whenever possible to deal with organizations capable of running several schools under a master contract. This would simplify the contract negotiation and monitoring problems faced by local school boards. Organizations responsible for several schools would be the local board's prime contractors. They would also become mechanisms to ensure school quality.

The local school board could create such organizations itself by entering into contracts with teacher cooperatives, teacher unions, local colleges and universities, profit-making firms, nonprofit civic and religious groups, and other local organizations to run multiple schools.

The board could also enter contracts with similar organizations established in other localities: a teacher cooperative in Minneapolis might agree to run some schools under contract with St. Paul. Ted Kolderie of the University of Minnesota has envisioned just such an arrangement as a long-term consequence of Minnesota's Charter Schools law, which lets a local school board designate existing school communities to "opt out" of the existing central administrative processes and labor laws.

As these locally based organizations develop capable staffs and managerial capacity, the ones with quality reputations might become regional or national in scope, offering to run schools in many school districts and providing assistance to other schools for a fee. At that point they would come to resemble existing contract-school providers, hereafter called "management and assistance providers" (MAPs). One existing MAP, Education Alternatives, Inc., develops curricula, trains teachers, provides quality control, and assesses performance for the schools it runs. Local school boards still make their own assessments of the schools' performance, but the basic work of maintaining product consistency and quality is done by Education Alternatives, much as, according to Celio (1995), it is performed by religious orders for Catholic diocesan school systems.

Organizations capable of running multiple schools can develop distinctive approaches to education and capitalize on the recognition and consumer confidence that a "brand name" engenders. They are also likely to benefit from economies of scale in designing curricula and in staff development. As Celio has shown, the stronger schools run by an organization can assist the weaker ones, and staff can be transferred from one school to another, both to shore up shaky programs and to increase exposure to high-performance organizations. Because of these advantages, schools operated by MAPs are likely to become major forces in a contract system.

The services of MAPs cannot be free. Their costs would be paid from contract funds received by the schools. A school might join a MAP for a fee, or a MAP running several schools could deduct its operating costs before sending money to the schools. Estimates of these costs vary. Catholic diocesan school systems typically assess schools between $10 and $25 per student to pay for testing, consulting, and financial management services. This compares rather favorably to the

$1,000 to $1,500 per student skimmed off by many big-city public school system central offices.

Assuming a school size of 500, a MAP charging $25 per student for services would cost the school $12,500. A secular organization might pay its employees twice as much and deliver more services than a Catholic diocesan school system, therefore requiring as much as $50 per pupil. If the average per-pupil expenditure were $5,000, the school's overall budget would be $2.5 million, and the MAP's costs would be 1 percent of the total. Another cost estimate can be based on the Edison Schools' rule of thumb that the corporate central office would have one staff member per 2,000 students. If the average school size were 500 students, that would make one staff member per four schools. If these staff members cost $100,000 each (salary, fringe benefits, and office overhead), the cost per school would be $25,000, again less than 1 percent of the school's budget.

Public officials would retain ultimate responsibility for school quality. They can replace contractors that fail to deliver, or force a MAP to make substantial quality improvements as soon as performance falls below acceptable levels. A local public education authority can also continually "prune" its portfolio of contractors. When contracts come up for renewal, contractors whose schools fall below some set level of performance (say the 25th percentile of all local schools) could be eliminated from consideration. The contracting system in fact ensures something that is not now possible in public school governance: unrelenting attention to the quality of instruction and learning in the lowest-performing schools. Contracting should, over time, substantially raise performance in the weakest schools and average performance levels of all district schools.

Quality Assurance

Contracting forces schools to say exactly what they hope to accomplish with their students, and it creates strong incentives for school staffs to assess their own performance and make a public case that they have succeeded. Parents and local authorities need not always accept schools' assertions at face value, but they can make school-provided information an integral part of the accountability process. Local public authorities will also need to develop their own measures of school performance, and ensure that parents have a full range of performance information on all schools. The result should be that everyone involved in public education—parents, school staffs, the public, and public education officials—will know much more about individual schools than they do now.

The choice of school performance measures and standards is critical to the success of a contract system. Performance measures and standards must be of two kinds: those that reflect the school's own particular instructional objectives and strategies, and those that permit valid comparison between schools and over time. The former measures should be part of a school's overall educational strategy, and thus be established in its contract. A career-oriented school, for example, aspires to outcomes that more academic schools do not seek, i.e., job placement in specific fields or admission to advanced skills-training programs. Other schools might frankly aspire to high scores on college placement tests and admission to competitive four-year colleges. Measures that permit valid comparisons among schools and over time must include student achievement tests, and they can be mandated statewide or locally by public education authorities.

As this is written, however, educators have little experience with school-specific performance measures. Public schools are not in the habit of assessing themselves or initiating public discussions of their performance. Public education agencies have developed testing programs that allow comparisons among schools, but these are insensitive to differences in schools' educational approaches or to differences in the prior educational attainment of students who attend particular schools.

For contracting to lead to real school-level accountability, school staffs must devise performance measures that are logically related to school-specific goals and methods. Schools will need to say what a student is expected to know and do at particular grade levels, and produce credible evidence of achievement. Student portfolios and live performances might be important elements of some schools' self-assessments. Schools that intend to affect students' attitudes or their capacity to contribute to the broader community will need to find ways of measuring and demonstrating results. Schools that send students on to other schools (e.g., from elementary to middle school, middle to high school, or high school to college) will need to find ways of tracking their own graduates' performance. Schools that intend to keep pace with similar schools elsewhere (e.g., schools specializing in science, mathematics, or classical education) can submit themselves to judgment by inspectors or accreditors who draw comparisons among schools with similar announced goals.

Very few public schools now do these things. Though a few public school principals are willing to be evaluated and take the consequences, most are convinced that evaluation is insensitive to school-specific needs and accomplishments. Feelings against evaluation are so high that few school staffs can sustain a discussion about how they would like to be evaluated. Most conclude only that they should be trusted to serve their students. In a contract system, however, school-specific evaluation is inevitable. If schools cannot say what they expect to accomplish, local education officials have no basis on which to establish contracts and carry out their responsibility to protect students. Schools that lack clear performance expectations are also defenseless if they become controversial or if small groups of parents or interest group leaders complain about them.

Real school-level accountability also requires cross-school comparisons. Student performances, portfolios, postgraduation experience, and accreditation can all serve this purpose if they are rigorously and fairly scored. But doing so requires benchmarks for portfolios and performances and equivalency of methods in tracking of graduates and in accreditation. Even if all these things are done, however, parents and public authorities will still want student test scores. There is no way a contract system can operate in the absence of student achievement test scores, including averages and ranges for all students, and for minority or low-income students, in every school.

Most states and many localities run student testing programs that can readily produce such information. No state or locality, however, now analyzes student test scores in ways that meet all the needs of a contracting system. Contracting requires a method of establishing specific reasonable expectations for every school. Under contracting, individual schools will be responsible for saying exactly what their students will achieve. Staff must take account of the effectiveness of their instructional approach *and* their students' degree of academic preparation. A potential school provider that promises very little will have a hard time winning a contract; however, a school that overpromises will quickly get into trouble.

For contracting to work, local education authorities must be capable of frank discussion with school contractors. What is realistic to expect in a school that serves a shifting population of new immigrants? If a contractor provides a school in a neighborhood where many resident students have, for years, failed to learn to read and dropped out in 9th grade, what is a reasonable performance expectation? How much improvement can be expected in a school that already has the best outcomes in the district? It may be good politics to say that all schools are expected to get steadily better and that every student is expected to meet statewide standards, but a contracting system that did not take account of student body and neighborhood needs would fail. Public authorities that imposed unattainable performance standards would either get no offers or be forced to deal with people who would promise anything to get a contract. Potential school providers who promised steady but gradual improvement would always lose the competition of promises.

The only solution is for school performance goals to be negotiated openly, in light of information about the range of real performance in schools of different types. In a given state or locality there is usually a small number of schools doing an especially good job with disadvantaged students, and others serving their own particular populations especially well. Such schools, or national benchmark schools, could be used as standards, and contractors could cast their proposals in terms of how quickly their students' performance would rise relative to high levels of performance observed elsewhere.

Today's public education system evades such frank discussions with rhetoric suggesting that it is unfair to expect less of some students than others. Many schools are evaluated on standards they cannot meet and then ritualistically condemned for failure, but nothing changes. In the long run, all students can indeed learn to high standards. But in the short run it is better to have well-thought-through plans and demanding but realistic expectations than to hope for magical solutions. Contracting makes it possible for local education authorities to choose realistic progress over extravagant rhetoric.

Once every school has a contract with tailor-made performance expectations, public education authorities have real leverage for quality assurance. The local public education authority will fulfill its responsibility for providing a quality education to all children by maintaining a portfolio of contracts serving two objectives: first, ensuring that the local system as a whole offers a range of approaches and services that matches the diverse needs of local children; and second, ensuring that no child receives a low-quality education.

Contractors that failed to provide instruction as promised, or whose students' outcomes were low and not improving as anticipated, could be fired or given an ultimatum to improve or be replaced. Parents could also take their children out of low-performing schools at any time and move them into better-performing schools. Local public authorities would be under an obligation to warn parents that a school had run into trouble. Authorities would also be obliged, by constant attention to their portfolio of contracts, to see to it that children leaving a failing school had a better place to go.

School superintendents and central offices would not wither away entirely. The local board would identify the need for particular kinds of schools, identify contractors potentially able to provide such schools, solicit proposals, and negotiate contracts. It would also continuously evaluate contractors' performance, both to prepare for negotiations around contract renewal and to identify contractors not delivering on their promises and failing to produce positive student results.

In communities where parents were intensely interested in choosing among schools, private organizations might make money selling information about schools. (One national information service, School Match, now offers data on school systems to business people thinking of relocating.)

However, as Chubb and Moe (1990) argue, public authorities must insure that all parents, not just the ones able and willing to pay, get such information. They suggest that the state fund independent parent information centers. Local public authorities would also need assistance in identifying needs for new types of schools, identifying promising potential contractors, and monitoring contract performance. Many of these functions could be performed by contractors, though not the same ones that operate the schools. But the processes of evaluation and contractor identification could not be neglected or performed for free; these functions would be the main mechanisms by which the public was assured that its children were being well cared for and its money carefully used.

Protecting Children from School Failure

Contracting must also offer protections for children whose schools fail despite all the pressures for high performance. Under contracting, parents can withdraw their children from a failing school instantly and enroll them somewhere else. However, the value of this remedy depends on the vigilance of parents and the availability of genuine alternatives. Inattentive parents may be slow to withdraw their children and inadvertently help prolong the life of a failing school. Parents in troubled areas of a city may also feel that there is no better alternative available within reasonable distance.

Some analysts think the problem of inattentive parents is a red herring. As Coons and Sugarman (1978) wrote, government can rescue children from flagrant parental abuse, but it has no power to guard them against parents' willingness to settle for second best. A government that tries to second-guess routine parenting decisions will inevitably do more harm than good. Still, many educators fear that ill-educated parents, or those impaired by substance abuse, will fail to pursue good choices, permitting bad schools to survive by catering to them.

Under contracting, parental choice is only one protection for children against school failure. The local public education authority can threaten to cancel the contract of a failing school, and the contractor, whether a single school or an intermediary organization, must respond successfully or lose its contract. The use of MAPs can also increase the options of local education authorities. The local board can assign a failing school to a MAP with a good track record. Some problem schools might even be doled out among MAPs as "assigned risks."

A MAP running a troubled school would also have many choices. It could fire or retrain staff and switch key staff members from its stronger schools. It can even bring in temporary "SWAT teams" of headquarters experts. As unusual as these steps might appear in the current governance system, Celio (1995) describes how some Catholic religious orders use all of them to improve school performance.

The success of the contracting system in dealing with school failure depends on the existence of a good supply of alternative providers. Contracting lowers the risks of starting a school by guaranteeing contractors a building, a fixed minimum income, and full reimbursement for all costs for students enrolled above the minimum expected number. It lowers entrepreneurs' front-end costs and guarantees their cash flow. Lower costs and fewer risks do not guarantee that entrepreneurs and social service agencies will offer to run schools, because even under these circumstances, schools will remain hard to run and profits may be elusive. But contractors need not fear the outright losses that market entrepreneurs face when they decide to open a school and nobody enrolls. Under contracting, organizations motivated by professional or social justice concerns could afford to try running schools. (Chapter Six will review the roles of states and federal governments and private organizations in ensuring a supply of competent school providers.)

CONCLUSION

Contracting has three major advantages over the current system. First, it creates positive performance incentives for school staffs. Second, it ensures that public funds are spent where they count, at the school level. Third, it deflects pressure for overregulation of schools.

Because contract schools would be schools of choice, a school would need to attract students in order to survive. It must therefore offer something that sets it apart—a distinctive curriculum, social climate, or extracurricular program. It must also provide a stable program that parents can rely on. The need for product differentiation encourages a number of behaviors that "effective schools" advocates have tried to create in public school staffs. Staffs would have a strong incentive to articulate a mission for the school and to ensure that all elements of the school contribute to its attainment. The mission must also be easy to explain to parents: that means it must be focused on what children will experience in school and what they will be able to do upon leaving it, not on subtleties of educational technique that may matter only to professionals. The demands of sheer economic survival will also make teachers concerned about the performance of the school as a whole.

Contracting creates strong pressures on public officials to maximize the share of funds spent at the school level and limit the amount spent on administration, regulation, and support of central decisionmaking processes. School contractors will know exactly how much money they have to spend, and therefore how much is skimmed off by the state or local central offices. School contractors will inevitably want as much money as they can get, and though they might become a force for higher overall education spending, they will also be strong critics of "taxation" for central office functions. Superintendents and central offices will have to explain where money goes and why things cost as much as they do. This is a profound change: school staffs now have no way of knowing how much money is spent on their school site, and central administrators can make unverifiable claims about how much of the money they control is spent on items the schools would otherwise have to purchase themselves. A contract school system may, in fact, have trouble spending enough for central oversight and evaluation. As Chapter Six will suggest, state laws authorizing contracting may have to require minimum levels of spending on school evaluation, assistance to new school providers, and public information.

Third, contracting would stabilize the rules that schools operate under. Public officials are now free to impose new requirements on schools at will: since nobody knows exactly how much money schools spend, or for what, it is hard to quantify the cost of a new mandate to add a course, write new reports, change staff assignments, or mainstream a group of students who before were served in a special program. From the perspective of public officials, such mandates are free, which is another way of saying that the costs are visible only at the school level. As principals and teachers in school systems in nominally site-managed school systems learned, public officials cannot resist imposing new requirements, even when they have promised not to do so. Contracts would specify all of a school's rights and obligations. Though officials might try to increase the number of "boilerplate" requirements in each new contract, school operators would be in a strong position to point out what new requirements cost and how they affect school productivity.

Chapter Five

CONTRACTING AND OTHER REFORMS

This study examined two other alternative governance concepts that have been widely discussed, one relying on free-market concepts, the other advocating reforms that would maintain the existing governance system but align all of its parts to support specific curriculum goals and student performance standards. The alternatives are, in brief:

- **Market competition.** Privately owned and managed schools, each operating under light government supervision, receive a fixed amount of public money for every student they enroll.

- **Standards and alignment.** Public agencies continue to own and operate schools, but the current system of multiple mandates is replaced by a more consistent and rational set of goals, performance standards, outcome measures, and rewards and penalties.

Advocates of both claim they would offer significant improvements over the current system. This chapter defines the two alternatives, identifies their strengths and weaknesses, and shows why contracting is superior to both.

MARKET COMPETITION

John Chubb and Terry Moe made the most complete case for market competition in their 1990 book, *Politics, Markets, and America's Schools.* But their case was only the latest and most complete in a series of books, arguments, and articles that advocated replacing the present heavy reliance on bureaucratic management of public schools with a lightly regulated market. As early as 1970, the Office of Economic Opportunity (OEO) tried to mount an experiment with education vouchers (see Jencks and Areen 1970; Areen and Jencks 1971). Since that time, lawyer John Coons and several collaborators have advocated introducing consumer choice and market discipline into public education (see especially Coons and Sugarman 1978). The immediate precursor to Chubb and Moe's book, *Winning the Brain Race*, was coauthored in 1988 by the CEO of Xerox, David Kearns, and the former OEO voucher experiment manager, Denis Doyle.

Since the 1970s, the movement led by Coons, Doyle, Chubb, and Moe has been represented by the term "choice." However, virtually all the major alternative governance concepts discussed in this report advocate greater choice in education. What set Chubb and Moe apart was their emphasis on private ownership of schools and transfers of public funds to parents in the form of scholarship vouchers. Though it is possible to create a system for parents to choose among publicly operated schools, Chubb and Moe wanted more than choice among public agencies: They advocated entrepreneurial freedom for private individuals and organizations to offer schooling in return for publicly paid tuition.

Chubb and Moe argue strongly for releasing schools from the dead grip of legislatures and government agencies. Unlike the alignment alternative described in these pages, however, Chubb and Moe envision a system completely divorced from public control. They write: "The schools' most fundamental problems are rooted in the institutions of democratic control by which they are governed; and despite all the talk about "restructuring," the current wave of grab-bag reforms leaves those institutions intact and in charge" (p. 216). They sketch out a publicly funded school system "that is almost entirely beyond the reach of public authority."

In the pure form proposed by Chubb and Moe, government has no relationship with schools, except to license them as private schools are now licensed and to provide subsidies that help parents pay their children's tuition. Government agencies would have no responsibility for staffing, supervising, or guaranteeing quality control in the schools. Market forces, and the self-interested initiative of people who own and staff the schools, are expected to efficiently meet public concerns with quality. Good schools would attract many tuition-paying students and make money. The best could not only sustain themselves but even expand or open new branches. Bad schools would attract few students and go broke.

The strengths of market competition as a solution to the current system's problems should not be underestimated. Schools in a free market, like schools in a contract system, would be forced to attend to student needs and parent preferences, rather than to the requirements of a centralized bureaucracy. Funding would be based on attendance, not on Byzantine processes of negotiation and the placement preferences of senior teachers. Teachers and principals would have strong incentives to collaborate, press one another for good performance, weed out weak staff members, and work as hard as necessary to build their school's clientele. Teacher pay and job security would depend on contributions to school performance, not on longevity or accumulation of credits and degrees.

Schools would compete for students, and in doing so they would be forced to differentiate their programs and products, both in quality and type. Some schools might try to be excellent in a safe, conventional way, while others would provide innovative services or appeal to particular tastes in subject matter or pedagogy. Product differentiation would help parents and students anticipate what to expect from a school. They would know whether they were likely to enjoy it and be willing to do the work it requires. They would also have little trouble knowing whether the school had kept its promises. Accountability would therefore be direct and immediate: Schools that delivered keep their students; those that did not would be abandoned. All in all, there is a lot to recommend the free-market approach.

STANDARDS AND ALIGNMENT

The idea of a system aligned to support specific learning goals comes from many sources. Former California schools chief William Honig introduced the idea of "systemic reform," careful matching of everything from curriculum to testing and teacher training, into that state's education system. The 1990 national education summit, called by President George Bush and attended by the governors of all the states, including Bill Clinton, endorsed education goals that were to drive a systemwide reform effort. The task of fleshing out the systemwide reform was taken up by a National Education Goals Panel, originally headed by Governor Richard Romer of Colorado. Analysts arguing for alignment-based reform include Marc Tucker of the National Alliance for Restructuring, and David Hornbeck, former chief state school officer in the state of Maryland and now superintendent of schools in Philadelphia. Hornbeck formulated a strategy for statewide governance reform in Kentucky, based on the concept of a rationally linked system of statewide goals, performance standards, examinations, and rewards and penalties for students and schools. Other important contributors to the concept are Marshall S. Smith and Jennifer O'Day of the Stanford University School of Education, allies of Honig's in propounding "systemic school reform," which built outward from strong curricular frameworks to align all parts of a state's education system.[1]

Alignment is not a total alternative to the present system, but an effort to make dramatic qualitative improvements in what is already there. The different proponents of an aligned system may disagree on some points, and they certainly start in different places: Hornbeck begins with statewide or national goals and deduces what is needed in curriculum, measurement, and accountability. Smith and O'Day would start with a consensus on curriculum and develop a system of governance and technical assistance to ensure its implementation.

Despite their different points of origin, however, alignment proponents share an important premise, and they come to very similar conclusions. The premise is that low-quality public schools are caused by confusion about the responsibilities of schools and diverse goals, means, and constraints that have emerged from multicentric political and administrative processes. The conclusion is that a more definitive set of goals, whether stated in terms of student outcomes or curriculum content, is the starting point for education reform. Once the goals are sharply defined, the other elements of the governance system can be engineered to meet them.

---

[1]In 1993, Smith was appointed Under Secretary of the U.S. Department of Education in the Clinton administration.

Alignment-based reforms affect the entire educational system, from the federal government down to the individual school. Hornbeck has developed models of "comprehensive statewide reform" for several states, including Washington, Ohio, Alabama, and Kentucky, where the ideas were first put together. The same comprehensive reform model also inspired the Nine Essential Elements of a Successful Education System, which the Business Roundtable has made the core of its 50-state education reform strategy. A national commission on the redesign of ESEA Chapter I also recommended that federal programs be alignment-based.

What does the alignment system look like in practice? An example of a state-level alignment effort can be found in the state of Washington. Washington's 1992–1993 reform thrust incorporates the following major elements:

- All the state's actions will be guided by clear and specific goals for student performance.

- The state will support a set of curriculum frameworks integrated with state goals and tests.

- The state will support tests and measures that provide school-level evidence on whether the goals are being met.

- Performance measures will trigger a range of responses to individual schools, including recognition, awards, technical assistance, and restaffing and redevelopment.

- Schools will be accountable for results, not compliance.

- A Quality Schools Center will function as a nonregulatory adviser and broker of technical assistance.

- The state will identify schools that exemplify good use of the standards and curriculum frameworks.

Alignment makes very explicit and uniform demands on schools. However, its main proponents are on record favoring school-level initiative. They expect clear goals, curriculum frameworks, tests, teacher training, and rewards and penalties to focus, but not control, the efforts of local teachers and school administrators. How the values of alignment and school-level initiative are to be reconciled is not clear.

Though alignment is a simple idea, its implementation can be complex. It is to be accomplished in part by major investments in training and resocialization of teachers, ensuring that their knowledge and professional values are consistent with the idea of a rich and challenging curriculum. Most of the states that have adopted comprehensive statewide reform bills have pledged a manyfold increase in budgets for teacher training, at least in the first few years after enactment. Alignment is also accomplished in part by enforcement, ensuring that low-performing schools are readily identified, and that teachers and administrators in successful schools are consistently rewarded and those in failing schools are either assisted or penalized.

PROBLEMS WITH THE ALIGNMENT AND MARKET SYSTEMS

Overall, the market system and alignment offer improvements over the current system in some ways. The market system, like contracting, is excellent for supporting initiative in schools and creating pressures for school performance. The standards and alignment system also creates strong pressures for school performance, and provides for aggressive state actions to force change in failing schools. Both have elements that are important to a contracting scheme—parent and teacher choice in the case of the market system, and definite frameworks for assessment of school performance in the case of alignment.

Because they have been widely discussed as potential reforms of the whole public education system, it is important that their weaknesses also be made clear. The remainder of this chapter will therefore emphasize the areas in which the market and standards/alignment systems fail to offer improvements over current public education governance arrangements.

Alignment

The alignment approach imitates current governance arrangements in treating the school as the lowest-level unit in a large hierarchical organization. The hierarchy of goals, standards, curriculum frameworks, and tests is intended to inform local professionals about what must be accomplished and to guide individual schools in setting improvement priorities. The school is governed by rules and standards, and is a franchise of the system's central office, not an enterprise of the teachers and administrators in it.

Despite its advocates' desire for greater school-level initiative and responsibility, alignment is unlikely to encourage such changes. Uniformity of teacher and principal training might lead to greater integration of effort within schools, but schools will still be driven by the need to comply with mandates created elsewhere. Although, in theory, there may be room for instructional innovation, schools whose students have trouble passing key state and national examinations and obtaining proposed "certificates of initial mastery" will have little choice but to concentrate on covering the materials in the examinations. Indeed, as Koretz (1988, 1991) has shown, teaching to the test always narrows the range of what is taught, even if the tests cover important materials. Schools confident of their students' ability to pass high-stakes tests can afford to spend time on information, issues, topics, and themes they consider important, whether or not they are part of the test. Other schools cannot afford that freedom.

The proposals for school delivery standards embodied in the Clinton administration's Goals 2000 Act further emphasize the centrality of compliance in an alignment system. Civil rights organizations and groups concerned with the education of disadvantaged students objected to the testing and certification required by a standards-based system, pointing out that all students will be held accountable for identical performance standards regardless of the quality of education they receive. Students who are, through no fault of their own, educated in impoverished or low-quality school systems will suffer. They will have less opportunity to learn what is required to pass the tests, and therefore will lose access to jobs and higher education. Service or delivery standards have been proposed as the solution to this problem. If all schools are required to deliver instruction that meets the same minimum standards (stated in terms of the methods and levels of instruction, student exposure to factual material, and practices using higher-order analytical skills), all students should have equal chances of passing high-stakes examinations and gaining skill certifications that lead to opportunities in employment and higher education.

Delivery standards will inevitably direct teachers' and administrators' attention to compliance issues. Schools whose students are in danger of failing key examinations will be forced to prepare a defense, and the only sure defense is the traditional one, compliance. A school whose instructional services meet the standards is free to take the attitude, "If students fail, it is not our fault." The pressure for compliance behavior is likely to be intensified by proposals to allow parents who felt their child's school failed to meet service standards to sue in federal court. Courts would be asked to rule on which services met which standards and on what exceptions to the norm were impermissible. State education agencies and enforcement units like the U.S. Department of Education's Office for Civil Rights would inevitably adopt court-developed standards as the basis for their own actions.

School staffs anxious to avoid litigation or administrative penalties would be handed the strongest possible incentive to follow what had been blessed in adversarial judicial processes and to make sure their services passed legal muster. (See Kimbrough and Hill 1981 for a discussion of similar processes occasioned by judicial decisions under the Education for All Handicapped Children Act.) There may be quicker ways to strangle school initiative in the cradle than state or local lawsuits, but if there are, they have not yet been discovered.

No one can be against clearer and more articulate goals and standards and a serious commitment to ensuring that all students get an education that can prepare them for the modern world. Taken in conjunction with genuine institutional changes, standards and alignment can lead to real reform. But grafted onto the current system of governance, alignment leaves key elements of the existing system intact, including comprehensive rule-making by school boards, other legislative bodies, and courts, and a detailed inspection and compliance process administered by permanent school system bureaucracies.

The fact that the curriculum framework is uniform and mandatory means that issues about it will inevitably become politicized. Even if its design is delegated to groups of specialists working with the public and educators in an effort to frame consensus, its authority will ultimately depend on legislative action. Faced with the demand either to mandate or forbid the teaching of some set of ideas, legislatures will be forced to choose between burdening schools with new requirements and finding verbal compromises that eliminate controversy by creating ambiguity.

This process—legislative control leading to disjointed mandates and avoidance of controversy—is the same one that produced today's fractionated and misaligned public school system. Schools operating under an official curriculum framework may be able to define clear missions and take distinctive stances in the beginning. Sooner or later, however, political pressures are likely to erode the curriculum framework, and the forces that now dominate public education governance will soon return it to its current form.

Alignment-based reform does not answer the question of how the political forces leading to fractionation are to be controlled. Smith and O'Day (1991) and O'Day and Smith (1992), for example, show how "a common vision and set of curriculum frameworks establish the basis in systemic curriculum reform for aligning all parts of a state instructional system," but do not show how that common vision will be created or stabilized in the face of diverse public ideologies, aspirations, and interests. Brandon (1993), writing of the difficulty of maintaining alignment in such a system, notes that

> each component presents . . . a moving target. . . . While a small group of reform leaders or coordinators will be examining the changes and interrelationships among all these moving components, most policies in each area will be determined by active and committed individuals whose attention is focused on one part of the picture. While [active and committed individuals] may be aware of the overall educational policy context in which they operate, it is difficult to conceive of a workable centralized process which would keep them all working within a coherent set of timeframes and limited missions (p. 9).

Alignment presumes a detailed consensus on what is to be taught, something Americans have not reached and are unlikely to reach soon. Alignment is a reasonable aspiration, and it is desirable to remove inconsistencies based on accident or habit rather than carefully worked-out settlements of political disputes. But the consensus for a fully standardized, rationalized, and coherent educational system is not likely to arise and, as Brandon writes, "if there is no consensus there is no reform." He suggests that standards and alignment is better considered a movement than a fully engineered reform. Those who believe a more coherent educational system will be more effective should organize to identify changeable inconsistencies, but they should not expect ever to reach a stable and complete alignment of all elements of the system.

The Market System

The market system offers a potentially strong remedy for educational failure: Parents can withdraw their children from a failing school instantly and enroll them elsewhere. The value of this remedy depends on two things: the vigilance of the parents and the availability of genuine alternatives. Inattentive parents may be slow to withdraw their children and inadvertently help prolong the life of a failing school that should be going broke. Parents in troubled areas of a city may also feel that no better alternative is available within a reasonable commuting distance.

Some analysts think the problem of inattentive parents is a red herring. As Coons and Sugarman (1978) write, government can rescue children from flagrant parental abuse, but it has no power to guard them against parents' willingness to settle for second best. A government that tries to second-guess routine parenting decisions will inevitably do more harm than good. Still, many critics of the market system fear that ill-educated or drug-impaired parents will fail to pursue good choices, and that some bad schools may survive by catering to them.

The real Achilles heel of the market system is the supply problem. The market system assumes that entrepreneurs, drawn by the possibility of lucrative tuition payments, would offer alternatives to unpopular schools. But it is not clear where alternatives to the existing bad schools are to come from. The alternatives do not exist now, and giving public school students access to the existing private and parochial school systems will not solve the supply problem. Even in New York City, where Catholic schools educate over 100,000 students and constitute what is in effect the 12th-largest school system in the country, there is no room for 1,000,000 public school students, or even one-quarter of that number. Few other cities or states have even that large a supply of privately run schools. An analysis of the 1993 California voucher initiative concluded that the state's existing private schools could expand only enough to enroll 4 percent of the students now in public schools (Dianda and Corwin 1993; Shires et al. 1994).

Starting or expanding a school is not cheap or easy. Aside from the capital costs of school buildings and equipment, the requirements of curriculum development, staff selection and training, and quality control are imposing. Whittle Communications' Edison Project will spend three years and tens of millions of dollars designing its new school. Edison expects to recoup its investment by opening a large number of schools and taking small profits from tuition in each, but the front-end costs are enormous. Despite its announced intention to charge tuition comparable to the average per-pupil expenditure of the nation's public schools, the Edison project is now raising tuition estimates and planning to use a great deal of time donated by parents and community members.

A weak private supply response may not be a serious problem in suburban and small-city school systems. Many such systems have essentially sound public schools that would almost certainly become more efficient and effective in the face of competition. Even the threat of competition clears the mind wonderfully, and might stimulate greater effort to make current schools more attractive to parents. The addition of a small number of private competitors has had a salutary effect in many small school systems.

But big-city systems have a different problem. Most of them have few schools that would be considered good by any standard. Many more big-city schools are failures by any standard. Some big-city systems already have a form of choice, in open-enrollment policies that allow students to enroll in any school with space for them. The opportunity to choose, however, has little meaning in the absence of a supply response. The demand for better schools has been apparent in big cities for a long time. But because no mechanism exists for starting new schools in response to demand, there is little evidence that the supply of good schools has increased at all. Until the 1994–1995 school year, when New York City started 50 new small high schools, the system's open-enrollment policy was virtually meaningless. The *nonselective* magnet schools to which all students may apply got 10 to 30 applications for every seat. The majority of students who tried to choose such a school ended up back in the school they tried to flee.

The rigors of education in big cities and all but the richest suburbs are likely to discourage most entrepreneurs. What profit-seeking entrepreneur could be confident in staying solvent running a school in an area burdened by violence, strikes, ill health, and family instability? What investor would choose to build a school in a core urban area when he or she might collect a similar amount per pupil in a far less stressed suburb?

Though critiques of a market system are stated in terms of equity and civil rights, they all reflect a concern for the supply problem. What member of the public would not want choice among schools if the public generally perceived that all schools were equally funded and most of them were pretty good places for children? The fact is that the public understands that all schools are not equitably supported and that many of them are quite dreadful educational institutions.

The fears that good schools will discriminate against the poor, and that children whose parents are not aggressive consumers will be consigned to the worst schools, are not figments of the public imagination. Those fears are well founded as long as the supply of schools is inelastic; that is, even though parents will have a greater capacity to demand good schools, if good schools are very scarce, the most important choices will be exercised by desirable schools, not the parents. Foes of a market system predict that schools will discriminate on admissions, grading, and teacher hiring, all to make themselves as attractive as possible to the middle class.

If good schools are in short supply, the market system is certain to generate charges of discrimination. No administrative agency will exist to disbar a school that suffers a scandal or to force quick action to remedy a problem. The result is that scandals of discrimination or malpractice will end up in the newspapers, courts, or legislative hearing rooms.

Should the facts bear out any of the fears outlined above, the market system is not likely to survive. Lawsuits based on unequal distribution of publicly funded benefits would lead to the imposition of new regimes of regulation. It is not far-fetched to think that schools accepting public funds would come under court-ordered regulation of their admissions, expulsion, grading, promotion, curricula, and teacher hiring and compensation. Chubb and Moe, and other market system advocates like Coons and Sugarman, admit that a market system entails these risks. They call for limited public regulation and oversight, including licensing of schools, to protect students and avoid devastating scandals.

COMPARING CONTRACTING WITH THE ALTERNATIVES

One can believe that the current governance system will work, but only under the assumption that school staff members can learn to take initiative and responsibility despite a structure of incentives designed to stifle it. One can believe that a market system will work, but only under the assumption that demand will spontaneously elicit a supply of schools that everyone, including the inner-city poor, can find worth choosing. One can believe that a standards and alignment system will work, but only under the assumption that a strong centrally administered system of rewards and penalties would not induce a compliance mentality at the school level.

The table below compares contracting with the two proposed reforms analyzed in this chapter, and with the current governance system. It rates each system on four issues used in Chapters Three and Four to analyze the current system and contracting, i.e., how well they support initiative-taking in schools, create strong pressures for high performance, stabilize the funding schools receive and the rules they must work under, and protect children from failing schools.

As Chapter Three argues, the current system does a poor job on all four criteria. The market system is excellent in supporting school

Table 1

Summary Ratings of the Alternative Governance Systems

	Present System	Market	Standards/ Alignment	Contracting
Support initiative in schools	Poor	Good	Poor	Good
Press for school performance	Poor	Good	Good	Good
Stabilize funding and regulations	Poor	Fair	Fair	Fair
Protect kids when schools fail	Poor	Poor	Fair	Good

initiative and pressing for high performance, as is contracting. Both make schools independent enterprises that control their own funds, staffing, and curriculum and that live or die on the quality of their performance. The success of the market system, however, depends on whether entrepreneurs offer an ample supply of good schools. If the supply response is weak, as is likely to happen in areas serving low-income and disadvantaged students, the market system will not protect all children from school failure and will be susceptible to reregulation.

Alignment improves on the current system by creating stronger and more consistent pressures for school performance, and by stabilizing funding. It also creates mechanisms for improving or replacing failed schools, but these are administrative and put high premiums on the performance of state education agencies. Moreover, unlike the market and contracting systems, it is susceptible to the return of "fragmented centralization," i.e., control of schools by uncoordinated mandates issued by courts, legislatures, and school boards.

Of the four alternative governance systems, only contracting stabilizes schools' funding and regulatory burdens and protects students when schools fail. It does the former by creating legally enforceable contracts that define each school's access to public funds and specifying the rules under which it must operate, and the latter by giving pubic authorities the power to cancel a failing school's contract and assign it to another, higher-performing organization.

There is, however, no need for communities or policymakers to choose only one pure approach to reform. Contracting includes many elements of the market system, and it is likely to work best when parents, teachers, and would-be school providers have the greatest freedom of action. Contracting also requires clear standard goals and credible objective methods of performance assessment, which current alignment-based efforts are struggling to produce. As Harvey (1994) has suggested, contracting and alignment might evolve into complementary reforms: contracting can contribute the school initiative and rewards and penalties for performance that can give real meaning to alignment's statewide goals, performance standards, and student performance measures.

A public school contracting system requires careful development and refinement. It is also sure to generate opposition from some entrenched provider groups. Like other potential revolutions in public policy, contracting can be watered down in the political process, to the point that all of the problems of the current system are recreated in it. The following chapter considers the problem of transition to a contracting system.

Chapter Six

MAKING CONTRACTING WORK

There appears to be a way to reinvent public education so that it encourages effective and initiative-taking schools rather than rooting them out. It would require massive changes in the ways schools are controlled, funded, staffed, and held accountable. Compared to the existing system and the alternatives discussed in this report, contracting is superior at encouraging initiative-taking and accountability, maintaining pressure for high performance, equalizing schools' opportunities to succeed, and intervening on behalf of children whose schools fail them. Contracting reduces local school boards' opportunities to micromanage and burden schools.

The question for this chapter is how to make possible serious testing and implementation of public school contracting. Reform of public education governance requires collaboration among state, local, and federal governments, and the serious commitment of local community leaders as well as educators. Education is for children, but it is delivered by adults. If Americans want better schools, the only way to get them is by changing the incentives and capabilities of the adults who teach and administer. The current system has tried to make schools answerable to everyone—to courts, civil rights enforcers, funders of categorical programs, school boards, central office administrators, regulators and civic leaders, and parents. The result, however, has not been the clarity of purpose that permits accountability, but the diffuseness of goals that breeds bureaucracy. If Americans want more effective and accountable public schools, we must reinvent the relationships between schools and all of adult society. This concluding chapter answers questions about the transition to contracting.

What actions must be taken by local community leaders and by the state and federal governments to make contracting possible? What practical arrangements are necessary for making the transition between the existing local governance arrangements and a new system based on contracting?

CHANGES AT THE STATE LEVEL

Amendments to State Law

Local education agencies are regarded as instruments of the state, and their powers and structure are defined in state laws and regulations. Many states limit local school systems' authority to contract out for services. The principle of treating teachers as civil servants, and collective bargaining rules that make unions into monopoly suppliers of teachers, are established in state law. Requirements that schools account separately for funds received from different sources, and for separate students and teachers who are covered by different grants, are encoded in state and federal regulations.

As Danzberger, Kirst, and Usdan (1992) argue, for schools to be governed differently at the local level, the state must redefine the role of the local school board and change the locus of control of money from the local central office to the individual school. They urge changes in state law to

- limit local school boards' responsibilities for settling disputes that could be resolved at the school level;

- relieve local boards of the burden of reaching collective-bargaining agreements with teacher unions;

- provide training and assistance to teach local board members about the importance of focusing on policy issues, not micro-management; and

- permit localities to select their own modes of governance, including leadership by elected or appointed boards, hired professionals, or other entities.

In most states, legislative action is necessary to enable local education authorities to contract out for the management of schools and to distribute cash, rather than staff and resources selected by the central office, to the schools.   State grant programs must also be amended to allow use of all state funds on a schoolwide basis, rather than for particular groups of students.   Changes in state labor laws are necessary to permit individual schools, not local education agencies, to employ teachers.   States with very large school systems, like New York, California, Florida, Texas, Michigan, and Ohio, may also need to redefine local education agencies so they serve smaller numbers of students and more compact geographic areas.   It may be possible for a local board to supervise contracts for 50 to 100 schools, but the complexity of doing so for several hundred, or a thousand in the case of New York City, is too great.   State legislation can be permissive: Some localities might choose to continue the existing mode of governance, while others (especially large urban districts where contracting offers a way out of a nearly hopeless situation) could choose reorganization and contracting.

Changes in Agency Missions

Contracting also requires changes in the missions of state education agencies.   Once local public education authorities are given the authority to contract for schools, the state would have three remaining roles:

•   help stimulate the creation and growth of organizations capable of serving as high-quality contract providers of schools;

•   provide statewide minimum standards for school performance and arrange for objective measurement and publication of school outcomes indicators; and

•   retain a capability to intervene in localities whose local education authorities fail to contract for an adequate supply of good schools or tolerate continued failure of particular schools.

The state role in stimulating a good supply of contract providers is critical.   In the absence of a continuous effort to increase the supply of qualified contractors, many localities might be forced to continue hiring the same small set of providers.   Though, as discussed earlier, school systems might choose to enter contracts with some existing school staffs, a local district without alternative providers might be forced to recreate via contracts what it already had. Local authorities with real options among contractors can demand good performance and fair prices. Authorities with few options would not be much better off than today's school boards, which must deal with a monopoly provider.

Scarcity of contractors will inevitably limit local authorities' options and reduce their leverage on contractors that are not performing well. A state government helping local districts implement a contracting-based reform should be driven by the aphorism coined by the Harvard Negotiation Project: In a negotiation, the party that has the advantage is not the one with the greater resources; it is the one with the best options (Fisher et al. 1991).

A serious state investment in contractor development, via small subsidies for new providers' start-up costs and efforts to identify and attract good MAPs working in other states, is needed to ensure that local education authorities have options. A state investment program, such as was attempted on the national level by the New American Schools Development Corporation (NASDC), should further enhance the supply. Oregon and Ohio have sought NASDC support for similar efforts at the state level.

As this is written, there are too few qualified contractors to go around. Several existing organizations are offering to manage multiple schools, including Education Alternatives, Inc., which now plays exactly that role in Baltimore and three other cities; the Edison Schools; Ombudsman Inc., which manages alternative high schools for troubled teenagers in several cities; educational reform networks run by Brown, Johns Hopkins, Yale, and Stanford universities; school design teams sponsored by the New American Schools Development Corporation; Ventures In Education, Inc.; and local religious systems including those directed by Catholic, Jewish, African American Protestant, and Lutheran organizations. Local education authorities that wanted to deal exclusively with MAPs would have to search for providers and entice some by promising long-term initial contracts. Authorities would also have to look carefully at providers' track records and watch their performance closely. But many potential providers exist, and most, especially the religious systems, would find the per-pupil funding available from local public authorities lavish and enticing.

State education agencies themselves might become contract providers. If states agreed to specialize in developing different types of schools—one state specializing in career-focused schools, another in schools focused on arts, classics, etc.—they could enhance the supply of providers for their own and others' localities. State education agencies would also have a continuing role to play in standard-setting and quality control. Though states need not create the kinds of exhaustive performance specifications required by the alignment approach discussed in the preceding chapter, they should continue establishing requirements for high school graduation and for performance of key measurable academic skills. Few localities have the R&D capabilities for such efforts, and many may be pressed, by parent groups and contractors, to lower their standards over time. The state government could countervail these forces by continuing to set graduation requirements. The state can also ensure that local education authorities and parents have good and unbiased information when they choose among contractors. Publication of performance data for every school and for every contractor (especially for contractors that operate in multiple districts) could ensure that local education authorities make well-informed decisions.

A system designed to produce educational diversity does not need and cannot use exhaustive standard measures of all aspects of school service delivery and performance. But it does need simple measures of school performance that are not closely linked to curriculum: student attendance rates, rates of credit accumulation, minority students' access to college preparatory courses, promotion and graduation rates, and graduates' rates of progress at higher levels of education and in their careers. Student testing is also desirable, but scores on available tests, such as the Preliminary Scholastic Assessment Test and the National Assessment of Educational Progress, might suffice.

Even under a contracting system, the state would unavoidably retain responsibility for protecting students. If the state took responsibility for providing comparative information about schools, it would avoid the danger, discussed in Chapter Four, that some local authorities would underinvest in such centralized functions in order to avoid criticism from contractors.

Collecting and publishing school performance data would give the state the information to identify local education agencies that were not replacing contractors despite poor performance, or that had, for an extended period, failed to find a contractor able to get good results in particular school sites. In such cases the state education agency could take a number of alternative actions: it could ensure that the local district knew about potentially more effective contractors, and it could determine whether the district was unable to attract better contractors because of spending limitations. If the local district were able to find better contractors and spend more but refused to do so, the state education agency could requisition the funds used for the failing schools and hire new contractors itself. If the district had too little money to hire high-performing contractors, the state could increase its funding for the affected schools, or for the district as a whole.

These functions require a state education agency of some size, and flexible funding to encourage start-ups of potential providers and to permit intervention in failing schools and districts. The state would not, however, need to maintain a large monitoring staff or pay directly for the extensive testing, staff development, and school improvement efforts required by the standards/alignment system. The state education agency's job would be to ensure that local education agencies have good options in contracting for schools, and that they use them.

Contracting requires state permission, but it need not be mandated for a whole state. Individual communities, especially big cities, could create enough demand to attract providers to run schools and to encourage additional organizations (e.g., teacher networks, teacher unions, and local universities) to organize themselves as school providers. From the perspective of the supply of potential providers, the more communities that adopt contracting the better. But contracting could work even if it were not adopted statewide.

CHANGES AT THE FEDERAL LEVEL

Though localities can contract for schools without the permission of Congress or the federal government, the structure of existing federal education grant programs could make contracting difficult. Except in very limited circumstances, the major federal grant programs,

Chapter I of the Elementary and Secondary Education Act and P.L. 94-142, the Education for all Handicapped Children Act, require recipient schools to single out particular students for special services. These requirements have a profound effect on school programs. As Kimbrough and Hill (1981) show, all of the instructional programs in a school are affected by the need to pull particular students out of their classes to receive federally funded services.

If contractors are to be fully in charge of their schools, and fully accountable for the results they obtain, they cannot be expected to work around fixed requirements for the use of particular funds for the instruction of particular students. Federal programs could be changed to make contracting possible, and contract schools could be required to show how disadvantaged students would benefit from the use of Chapter I funds and how the needs of handicapped children would be met by their instructional program. Contract schools could also be required to prove that such promises were kept, subject to loss of eligibility for future contracts. But they should not have to follow procedures invented for the kinds of highly regulated schools that prevail today.

MAKING THE TRANSITION AT THE LOCAL LEVEL

Taking Advantage of New Legal Authorities

State and federal law can open the door to local governance reform, but local actors must walk through it. The consensus-building and experimentation necessary for a revolution in local educational governance must start at the local level. Recent experience makes it clear that governance changes mandated by state law are unlikely to work exactly as intended at the local level. The Chicago example is instructive. The Illinois state legislation that initiated the Chicago school reform mandated creation of elected site councils and a movement to site-based management. But it could not account for the staying power of the Chicago public school central office, the Balkanization of the school board, the intransigence of the teacher union, or the board's failure to hire a superintendent who understood and supported the reform. The changes mandated by the state law were made, but they resulted in little fundamental change in educational governance. Local site councils found that they had the powers directly granted by the law—i.e., to hire and fire their principals—but they still had no control over their school's staffing or instructional and staff development programs. If poorly designed and weakly implemented, a governance reform based on contracting might produce similar disappointments.

Once local public authorities are allowed by the state to run all their schools via contracts, how can the new governance system come to work at the local level? Communities could move toward contracting incrementally. It will take time for school boards to identify potential contractors and develop contracts that give schools freedom but ensure accountability, and for contractors to hire staff and prepare instructional programs. In most localities it would take at least a year to put even a few contract schools into operation. The pace of contracting could be accelerated if local authorities adopted a policy of equal per-pupil funding and entered formal contracts with the principals and lead teachers of their best-performing magnet and specialty schools. The local school board could also commission groups of teachers and administrators to develop plans for new schools to be run under contract. Dade County, Florida used this method to develop the new "Saturn" schools, in response to enrollment growth in the late 1980s. Most of these schools became ordinary neighborhood schools, but some became notable magnet and specialty schools with de facto contracts. Once such schools were established, they could be given status as independent legal entities and enjoy the same freedoms and obligations as schools run by local nonprofits or MAPs.

Many localities have already made a start toward contracting via the charter schools process. Charter schools laws, now on the books in Minnesota, California, Wisconsin, Massachusetts, Michigan, Colorado, and Georgia, allow states and local districts to license quasi-independent public schools. Such schools can receive public funds and admit students currently attending regular public schools, but they are not bound by all the normal regulations and union contract provisions.

The original motivation for charter schools was to permit innovative educators and disaffected school communities to "opt out" of the regular public school system. Teachers, administrators, neighborhood groups, and educational innovators could apply for charters and begin operating highly distinctive schools. The first charters were typically run by innovators hoping to try out a new idea, but some charters granted in the past year have allowed existing schools to adopt new curricula, staffing plans, and teacher job descriptions.

Charter laws create a way around the existing system, but they are not intended to replace it. Local school boards do not initiate charter arrangements: they must wait for educators or community groups to propose charters, and then evaluate proposals via processes that put the burden of proof on those who would leave the existing system. Once a charter school is authorized, students can be admitted under processes specified in the charter. The school continues operating until the local board revokes its charter, the charter expires, or voluntary student attendance falls below the level required to pay operating costs.

In localities where community leaders wanted to move toward contracting, existing charter schools could be given real contracts and independent legal status. Local education authorities could also aggressively encourage additional groups to propose charters.

Charter schools laws, however, do not permit everything that a contracting system requires. Local authorities do not have the power to organize charters or to assign charter organizations to take over failing schools. Unless local authorities can initiate contracts via requests for proposals or direct negotiations with potential providers, contracting is unlikely to become any locality's dominant method for providing schools.

Though contracting is meant to be a whole system of alternative governance, it will inevitably work for a time as part of a hybrid system. Even in localities that were committed to contracting for every school, there will be a time in which some schools are operated under contract and others could still be governed under the current model. A hybrid governance system would require reductions in the local central office, to ensure that contractors actually received the full local per-pupil expenditure for each student they enrolled. As the number of schools run under contract increased, the central office could be gradually disbanded, and an infrastructure of independent support organizations would arise to sell services to schools. As has happened in the few school districts that have allowed their schools to buy services on the open market, most have found private providers of equipment, repairs, testing, instructional advice, and staff training more efficient than bureaucratically organized central offices.

Political Strategy

For contracting to take hold at the local level, strong local political organization is necessary. The impetus for fundamental governance reform is not likely to come from the people who work within the current system. The contending interests—board, union, superintendent, central office, taxpayer groups, federal and state monitors—usually operate in an equilibrium that none of them can change much. Even those who may be free to do their job better under contracting—especially teachers and administrators—may oppose it in preference to familiar patterns. A board election or change in superintendent can sometimes upset the equilibrium. But change frequently starts with the entry of new forces from outside the normal "iron triangle" of school board, superintendent, and teacher union: in the courts in many places; the business community, as in Cincinnati; and foundations and broader public interest organizations, as in Chicago.

External forces change the political equation. They create new ideas that are different from those advanced by the interest groups normally concerned with public education, and they broaden the set of actors whose interests have to be considered. As the present author argued in a report on how six cities mobilized to begin school reform (Hill, Shapiro, and Wise 1989), superintendents can become change agents, but they normally need the support of external forces like the business community. Those external supporters must stick with the change for a long time: if they become disinterested, the old equilibrium will quickly return. A standard "stakeholder" strategy, in which a potential leader tries to exhort and bargain with the established interest groups, cannot create profound reform.

A fundamental governance change can happen only if community forces of great power are organized to demand and sustain it. Mayors and top business leaders, who can define civic priorities and undertake projects as vast as downtown redevelopment and economic restructuring, must provide leadership for education governance changes. Grassroots campaigns to excite parents and community members—especially in minority communities, whose students are so poorly served by today's public schools—provide important support for governance changes. But committed leadership and continued problem-solving by the most senior local leaders are essential.

Once local leaders are committed to reform, the best way to move a local school system toward contracting is to use it as a way of improving education in neighborhoods where the existing public schools have failed. As the present author has suggested for Los Angeles, a policy of redeveloping the worst 5 percent of a city's schools via contracts each year would be a sensible approach toward full adoption of a contract system. It would give time for providers to learn their business and gain reputations. It would also permit the local education authority to learn how to act as a contracting agency and demonstrate the advantages of a free labor market to teachers and administrators. After one or two years, the next-lowest-performing 5 percent of the system could be replaced with contract schools, and on until the entire system was under contract.

A transition from partial to full use of contracting will also leave time for analysis of unexpected problems and for current and potential future superintendents to relearn their jobs. The superintendent's job will change profoundly: it will not be a school administrator's job at all, but the job of managing a lean but competent organization that controls the funds for a system of contract schools.

Most incumbent superintendents are understandably loyal to the system and the people who have served it, and are not now ready to do all that is necessary to bring about such a reform. A period of transition can give superintendents a chance to adapt (or to prove that they cannot adapt) and leave time for possible future superintendents to learn how to perform a transformed role.

Transforming Teacher Labor Relations

Contracting requires changes in the terms of employment for teachers and in the roles of teacher unions. Teachers will become independent professionals selling their services to schools. Unions will become brokers who help match teachers and schools and who counsel and train teachers who have difficulty finding and keeping jobs.

National union leaders have anticipated such changes (see, e.g., Shanker 1990), but some local leaders are not likely to welcome them. Contracting would force changes in the roles and powers of local union leaders themselves, and that would put particular pressure on the highly paid senior teachers whose interests the local unions most effectively represent. Local union leaders will run service agencies, not industrial unions with great bargaining power. Senior teachers will have to compete for jobs in a labor market where high salaries come with heavy responsibility.

Crippling teacher strikes are possible, but not inevitable. Properly introduced, contracting can gain widespread teacher support and isolate intransigent local union leaders and senior teachers who cannot or will not produce excellent work to justify high pay. Teacher associations can play extremely important roles in a contract system. As Ted Kolderie has suggested, union-initiated teacher cooperatives might offer to run whole schools. Groups of teachers from a specialty area (science, mathematics, literature, etc.) could organize to deliver specialized instruction in several schools. A good teacher cooperative might expand to run several schools, and even seek contracts from school districts in other cities or states. Teacher groups that gained good reputations could also provide summer services for their members by offering summer and evening classes or adult education, both under contract and for tuition.

Contracting could help teacher unions become true professional organizations, dedicated to improving the skills and job opportunities of their members, rather than to industrial strife. Current local leaders may resist such changes, but all localities have potential teacher leaders who would know what to do with the opportunity that contracting presents.

Local reform leaders may also need to develop alternative sources of teacher supply. As Grissmer and Kirby (1991) has demonstrated, most big states and metropolitan areas have ample supplies of certified teachers who have left the field but would be glad to reenter it. The market and contracting reforms would also instantly expand the pool of eligible public school teachers to include bachelor's degree holders in fields other than education, who make such a contribution to private schools' teaching of "solid" subjects like mathematics, science, and literature.

Good working relationships with teacher organizations will be important in reformed school systems, as they are now. But conflict is likely in the short run, and local public authorities can gain leverage if they ensure that governance changes expand the potential supply of teachers to include anyone who can teach well, not just those who are currently teaching.

Investing in Training and Development

A new governance system and its attendant expectations for performance require that teachers and administrators have time to learn how to work effectively. When a new school is started under contract, teachers accustomed to working in conventional public schools will need a period of adjustment. In a knowledge-based activity such as a K–12 education, there is no substitute for front-line workers' figuring out how to do things and acquiring new skills. As one former business executive has written, "As a CEO I worked for years learning how to do what I was already paid to do" (Carver 1990). As Senge (1991) points out, high-performance organizations do more than implement what is known: they learn how to do things that no one has ever done well before.

Educators naturally put great emphasis on training. But a governance change does not necessarily require a fully worked-out training program to ensure that everyone will be taught exactly what he or she must know. A change must create incentives for professionals to learn and adapt. Some adaptations require trial and error, and others require searches for examples and formulas. If the latter are readily available, professionals should at least be told where they can get appropriate training. But the advocates and designers of a contracting system cannot and should not act as if they are responsible for thinking of everything. Contracting puts money into the schools, money that can be used to buy consultants and training and to use school staff time to search for ways to run a successful school. Schools also gain the ability to replace staff members who cannot or will not learn to change. MAPs and networks of allied schools can also help school staff learn what is known about their problems and figure out the rest.

In Chicago and other school systems that have made governance changes, teacher groups have complained that implementation was impossible because "they [meaning senior public authorities] didn't give us the training." Some such complaints may be justified, but they can also be efforts to evade responsibility. The purpose of governance reform is to create conditions that allow teachers to be responsible for what they do and what their children learn. Complaining about a lack of training can be a way to rebuild the previous situation, in which teachers are responsible for compliance, not results. If governance reform is real, teachers and others in the schools will have the strongest possible incentive to figure out how to do their work: their jobs will depend on it.

Making Changes Stick

Reform is threatening, and educational interest groups have learned to play hard at politics. Those who would change the educational system must be equally firm and astute. Change requires more than good new ideas. It requires the elimination of existing structures and habits contrary to those ideas. That is not common practice in education. Reforms are typically seen as a marginal addition to the ongoing system, not as its replacement.

In implementing a new governance system, it is as important to decide what must be gotten rid of as to say what will be new. Changes must hit budgets, organizations, and people. There is no such thing as a hold-harmless reform. Organizational units and budget lines that are diminished but not eliminated constitute a shadow government that can return quickly if the reform falters. As Chicago reformers learned, an organization designed to do business in the old way does not adapt well to fundamental reform. When Chicago adopted a radical decentralization plan, reformers severely cut the central office budget but did not eliminate or change the mission of key administrative units. Although the central office was grossly understaffed, it still tried to perform all the same functions as before. The result was that schools were still subject to the same compliance reviews as before, and actions requiring central office convenience took even longer to process.

Real governance reform requires changes in the mission and structure of the whole school system. People whose jobs depended on the old system should not be given critical positions in the new structure. People should be pensioned off or reassigned to operating units away from any central management of the reformed system. Most central office administrators are qualified to work in schools, and many might start schools or go to work for MAPs. Central office employees who deliver staff development or plan curricula for the whole district can also set themselves up as private consultants or contractors, providing help to schools that choose to buy it.

It will take years before a new governance system will run smoothly. There will be problems and turbulence. Unless the senior and local civic and business leaders whose initiation was required to start the reform stay engaged, the new governance system will collapse or be distorted to serve ends other than those originally intended.

The changes contemplated in this report are unprecedented in American public education, so there is no way of predicting exactly how school board members, superintendents, principals, or teachers will do their jobs. The appendix presents one vision of the complementary roles of public authorities and school staff members, drawn from a series of focus groups conducted with Chicago parents, teachers, and principals in May and June 1992.

CONCLUSION

An effective and accountable public school system may be possible even in big cities where many citizens and educators have virtually given up. It will take profound and unstinting work to change schools, the employment conditions of teachers, and state, local, and federal education agencies. Many teachers and school-level administrators will have to learn new skills and scramble to keep their jobs, and many central office administrators will inevitably lose theirs, as might the leaders of local teacher unions unless they find new missions to perform.

Contracting is no panacea, and its use will inevitably bring some unpleasant surprises. But it is a plausible alternative to the current system, and it gives parents, citizens, and public officials a way of handling problems that have defeated educational policymakers. Leaders in any locality where people are asking, "Can the public schools be saved?" have little choice but to try it.

SUPPORT FUNCTIONS IN A REFORMED SCHOOL SYSTEM

Paul Hill, Barbara Holt, Paula Wolff, and Sara Spurlark

INTRODUCTION

The Chicago school reform plan contemplates sweeping changes in how schools serve children and how adults work together on students' behalf. But after three years of massive changes at the school level, little has changed in the administrative structure that is supposed to help schools function effectively.

Recognizing that it is time for reform to reach the school system's central office, the Chicago School Finance Authority (SFA) asked that a representative sample of principals, teachers, and local site council (LSC) members identify what services schools need and how they can best be provided. The starting point for the discussions was an agreement that the administrative and instructional system in the Chicago public schools must be child-centered. Further, authority and responsibility must be linked at the school level so that teachers and principals can achieve the goals of their School Improvement Plans. The product of the discussions, summarized in this paper, is the design of a support system for the schools in which some form of central office provides some but not necessarily all services needed by the schools.

This paper was written in 1992 at the conclusion of a series of focus groups in which principals and local site council members discussed what they hoped the Chicago public schools' central office would provide—and stop providing—for their schools.

This design establishes a series of principles but does not give a detailed implementation plan with personnel or budget analysis. Given the high level of complexity of the present central office organizational structure and budget, it is neither prudent nor practical for this group to make technical decisions about specific reallocations. We anticipate that the SFA, if it accepts these recommendations, will work with the board and central office as operations experts develop an implementation plan.

Our discussions began with the question of what services were essential to creating first-rate schools and then asked how these services could be provided. The focus groups did not start with the existing central office structure, but asked which functions should be eliminated or preserved. The discussions were not constrained by existing labor agreements. All participants, including teachers, principals, and parents, agreed that a reformed system might require a change in existing contracts over time.

The organization of this paper reflects our main conclusions. It starts with a number of conclusions about the character of a reformed school system and the roles of schools, central administration, and the general superintendent. It then summarizes the group's findings on how particular services should be provided. It ends with suggestions about a transition strategy—how we are to move from the current centralized school system to one that truly encourages and relies upon school-level initiative—and final observations.

GENERAL CONCLUSIONS

The most fundamental conclusion that emerged from the discussion is that the central office does not perform well many of the functions required for a reformed school system. This statement is true despite the earnest efforts of many competent people. Today's central office was built to manage a centralized bureaucratic system. For a reformed system based on school-level initiative and responsibility, many of the things the central office does are unneeded or harmful; many of the things the schools need, it does not do.

The central office's mission and structure need to be rethought from the ground up. There is no point in asking what will be the responsibility of a given unit or person within the current structure. The only plausible course is to determine first what needs to be done, and only then to ask who shall do it.

The second general conclusion is that the resources of the school system must be allocated directly to the schools whenever possible, and in the most flexible form possible. Very little money should be set aside for central office use. Resources allocated to the schools should be fungible, not earmarked for specific uses, wherever possible. The central office's uses of funds should be clear and understandable to all, and most central office services should be sustained only if schools confirm their value by purchasing them.

The third general conclusion is that the new administrative system must avoid creating new monopolies in service provisions. To the degree possible, schools should have access to multiple providers of all services, including private and nonprofit sources. The school system itself may offer some services, but these should not rule out private providers. The number of people permanently employed at the central office should be very small. To minimize the number of permanent central office organizations and staff members, the people who perform coordinating or brokering functions (e.g., helping schools identify possible providers of staff development, etc.) should be selected from among teachers or principals and should return to the schools after performing those services for a set term.

The final general conclusion concerns the role of the general superintendent. His or her role in a reformed school system is critical, but very different from that of today's superintendent. In the short run, the superintendent's job is to manage the transition from a bureaucratic system to a reformed one. His or her constituency is the schools and the children they serve, not the staff or bureaus of the central office. The superintendent should drive resources and responsibility into the schools, and initiate the elimination of organizational or contractual factors that impede reforms. The school board, understanding this to be the superintendent's role, must offer steadfast support, even when established interests are aggrieved.

In the long run, the superintendent's job is to protect children and find help for failing schools. School communities—principals, teachers, and LSCs—have the immediate responsibility for educating children. But schools are not sovereign, and their autonomy is conditional on performance. The superintendent must retain the power and the ability to intervene when individual schools prove unable to motivate and prepare their students. The superintendent should identify failing schools (based on standards established in the Reform Law and the State Report Card) and find help for them. Help need not come from a permanent central office establishment. The superintendent may rely on universities, consultants, and other independent sources.

The superintendent will not be able to carry these responsibilities without a staff. He or she may employ a small number of assistants (but far fewer than the number of schools to be assisted) and organize their work on any basis (e.g., geographic area or level of schooling) the superintendent deems appropriate.[1] Consistent with the principles outlined above, however, such staff members or organizational units must serve only at the superintendent's pleasure.

HOW FUNCTIONS SHOULD BE REALIGNED

This section provides detail on how particular services should be provided to the schools. It establishes several principles and guidelines, which will require careful further development and implementation. A subsequent section on transition strategy suggests how to create a process by which these principles can be put into action.

In-Service Training

If schools are to become cohesive and effective organizations, they must have responsibility for the development of their staff. To make this possible:

- Staff development funds should be allocated directly to schools on a per-pupil basis.

---

[1]The subdistrict superintendents incorporated in the reform legislation do not now serve a clearly understood or consistent function. Schools should be free to purchase the services of subdistrict offices or cluster together to form subdistrict "peer panels" for assistance, but no central office citywide services funds should be set aside for creating subdistricts.

- All funds now used for professional development bonuses should be allocated to schools.

- Both funds referred to above should be used to support the individual needs of schools as reflected in their school improvement plans, though schools may also decide to allocate some professional development funds to support individual teachers' aspirations.

- Schools should be free to buy help from each other, the central office, universities, or other consultants.

School Performance Assessment

School staffs must focus their attention on student growth. Every school community must continually ask, "Is this the best we can do for our children?" Answering that question requires that schools take the initiative to assess their own performance. Schools forfeit this initiative only when they demonstrably fail their students. To make this possible:

- State tests should be the only citywide standard assessments.

- Individual schools should be free to choose other measures, whether diagnostic or growth, if they wish.

- Contractual assessment services may be purchased from the central office or elsewhere. Schools may also form alliances for the purpose of reviewing one another's programs and results.

- The board should consider hiring contractors to perform periodic assessments of systemwide performance.

- The superintendent or the state must retain the authority to intervene in obviously failing schools, providing new staff or other resources necessary to restore the school's competence and autonomy.

Curriculum Development

School-level responsibility means that choices of textbooks, curricular emphasis, schedules, and methods of pedagogy must be tailored to students' needs. Schools should have the initiative, within broad guidelines, to define their own programs. To make this possible:

- Curriculum planning for individual schools should be limited only by state curricular standards.

- The design of each school's curriculum should be established by and its success measured against its capacity to meet state standards and the goals of the school implementation plan.

- Schools should be free to purchase assistance from the central office, state, universities, or other qualified vendors.

Teacher Credentialing and Hiring

Teachers should work for individual schools, not for the central office. Schools should be able to select teachers who complement the skills and approaches of existing staff. To make this possible:

- The system should maintain a list of eligible teachers who have passed the necessary screening and certification.

- School principals, in collaboration with department chairs and other teachers, should hire teachers on annual contracts. Interviewees may come from the eligible list mentioned above or from among other qualified teachers identified by the principal.

- Neither principals nor teachers should have site tenure.

- Teachers whose contracts are not renewed by their school would be returned to the eligibility list.

- Due process principles should be followed whenever a teacher's contract is not renewed for any reason.

Budgeting and Accounting

It is critical that schools control their budgets. To make local budget control and fiscal accountability possible:

- All funds not necessary to perform those functions recommended to be retained at the central office should be allocated directly to the schools on a per-pupil basis.

- The use of money not allocated to schools should be clearly explained in the budget.

- All school budgets should be finalized and approved by the central office before the beginning of the school year and then reconciled in a post-audit by the second week after the end of the school year. All spending during the school year is strictly the province of the school. Post-audit findings would be reconciled with the school and disparities settled through the next year's budget allocation.

- The central office would make available accounting services for individual schools that request them.

- There would be a small central "emergency fund" for schools in need of more resources than initially budgeted, but sanctions would be imposed in the next year's budget for use of these funds unless the emergency drawdown were deemed necessary by the general superintendent.

- Salaries for principals and building engineers should be set respectively by the LSCs and the principals, based on performance, not *size*, of school. The general school budget funds should be available for this purpose.

Building Repairs and Facilities Services

The schools must have control over their own day-to-day maintenance operations, with personnel reporting to the principals and resources for immediate repairs and maintenance in the annual budget. To make this possible:

- Funds should go directly to the schools.

- Engineers should be hired by principals off eligibility lists from the central office. All other functions should be contracted on a free-market basis, unless principals wish to employ full-time personnel to work in the schools. Such personnel would be off a central office eligibility list.

- There should be a separate capital fund for major repairs and renovations, allocated by the central office. Procedures and priorities for its use should be clear and open.

- Long-term physical plant planning should be done centrally, through an open process, using the best demographic projections and the advice and information from LSCs about the needs of their communities.

Mandated Services

Nothing in the reform strategy was meant to relieve schools of special responsibility to serve the disadvantaged, the handicapped, or students of limited English proficiency. Schools must take the initiative to meet such student needs and to demonstrate that the beneficiaries of federal and state categorical programs are appropriately served. To make that possible:

- Schools should have the initiative in saying how they will comply with rules and meet special needs.

- No school may reject special-needs students.

- The burden of proof of noncompliance should be on federal or state monitors.

- Central office federal program coordinators should be advisers, not supervisors.

- Federal Chapter I funds should be used on a schoolwide basis wherever possible.

TRANSITION STRATEGY

These changes should be made very soon. The first step is to have the central office make a complete accounting of all the resources of the school system and create a capacity to distribute all funds except those permanently retained by the central office directly to school accounts. Until this is done, no school community can be fully responsible for its own program or use of resources.

Schools should be allowed to volunteer to become part of the realigned system in September 1992. Schools not volunteering now must participate starting no later than September 1995. In the transition, the central office must allocate the full per-pupil value of all services (except those retained for the general superintendent's office, payroll, teacher personnel, warehousing, purchasing, and transportation) directly to the participating schools. The central office must make a full and explicit accounting of the use of all retained funds, and the allocation of the resulting benefits among the schools.

The movement toward realigned administration will be developmental. The process must be closely monitored and evaluated, preferably by an independent organization that can analyze progress delays, extract lessons from experience, and identify sources of resistance to full implementation.

FINAL OBSERVATION

The process that created these recommendations was unprecedented in American public education. The results reflect the needs of school community members who have worked hard to improve their own schools. Like many other elements of the Chicago reform, the changes recommended here are unprecedented in breadth and scale. Much remains to be learned. There may be false starts and localized failures.

Reform creates risks for everyone. The superintendent, the board, and the school finance authority all run the risk of having to change established routines, and change them again if the first effort does not succeed. Teachers and principals assume real responsibility for their schools and will be exposed to criticism if they misuse public funds or fail to meet the needs of children. But that is right. The current system puts children gravely at risk every day. Under these circumstances, there is no way to insulate the adults in the system from the risks of change.

BIBLIOGRAPHY

Areen, Judith, and Christopher Jencks. "Education Vouchers: A Proposal for Diversity and Choice." *Teachers College Record,* Vol. 72, 1971.

Bimber, Bruce. *School Decentralization: Lessons from the Study of Bureaucracy.* Santa Monica, CA: RAND, 1993.

Booz-Allen & Hamilton. *Financial Outlook for the Chicago Public Schools.* Prepared for the Civic Committee of the Commercial Club of Chicago. Chicago, 1992.

Brandon, Richard N. "Sustaining Political Support for Systemic Education Reform." Human Services Policy Center, University of Washington. Prepared for the Pew Forum on Education Reform. Working Draft, January 1993.

Breneman, David W. "Where Would Tuition Tax Credits Take Us? Should We Agree to Go? *Public Dollars for Private Schools: The Case of Tuition Tax Credits,* Thomas James and Henry M. Levin (eds.). Philadelphia: Temple University Press, 1983, pp. 101–114.

Carver, John. *Boards That Make A Difference: A New Design for Leadership in Nonprofit and Public Organizations.* San Francisco: Jossey-Bass nonprofit sector series, 1990.

Catterall, James S. "Tuition Tax Credits: Issues of Equity." *Public Dollars for Private Schools: The Case of Tuition Tax Credits,*

For more information on RAND publications or to order documents, see RAND's World Wide Web URL, http://www.rand.org/ RAND documents may also be ordered via the Internet: order@rand.org/

Thomas James and Henry M. Levin (eds.). Philadelphia: Temple University Press, 1983, pp. 130–150.

Celio, Mary Beth. "Building and Maintaining Systems of Schools: Lessons from Religious Order School Networks." Seattle: University of Washington Graduate School of Public Affairs, working paper, 1995.

Center for the Study of Public Policy. *Education Vouchers, A Report on Financing Elementary Education by Grants to Parents.* Cambridge, MA: CSPP, 1970.

Chubb, John E., and Terry M. Moe. *Politics, Markets, and America's Schools.* Washington, D.C.: The Brookings Institution, 1990.

Cohen, D. K., and E. Farrar. "Power to the Parents? The Story of Education Vouchers." *The Public Interest,* Vol. 48, 1977, pp. 72–97.

Coleman, James. "Toward Open Schools." *The Public Interest,* Vol. 20, No. 9, Fall 1967.

Commission on Chapter I. "Making Schools Work for Children in Poverty: A New Framework." Prepared by the Commission on Chapter I, U.S. Department of Education, December 10, 1992.

Coons, John E., and Stephen Sugarman. *Education by Choice: The Case for Family Control.* Berkeley, CA: University of California Press, 1978.

Cooper, Bruce S. "School-Site Cost Allocations." Paper presented at the general meeting of the American Educational Finance Association, 1993.

Crain, Robert, et al. *The Effectiveness of New York City's Career Magnets.* Berkeley, CA: The National Center for Research on Vocational Education, 1992.

Dansberger, Jacqueline, Michael Kirst, and Michael Usdan. *Governing Public Schools: New Times, New Requirements.* Washington, D.C.: Institute for Educational Leadership, 1992.

Darling-Hammond, L., A. E. Wise, and S. R. Pease. "Teacher Evaluation in the Organizational Context." *Review of Educational Research,* Vol. 53, 1983, pp. 285–328.

Darling-Hammond, L., and A. Wise. "Teaching Standards, or Standardized Teaching?" *Educational Leadership,* Vol. 41, No. 2, 1983, pp. 66–69.

Davies, Howard. *Fighting Leviathan: Building Social MarketsThat Work.* London: The Social Market Foundation, 1993.

Davis, Evan. *Schools and the State.* London: The Social Market Foundation, 1993.

Dianda, Marcella R., and Ronald G. Corwin. *What a Voucher Could Buy: A Survey of California's Private Schools.* Los Alamitos, CA: Southwest Regional Laboratory, 1993.

Doyle, Dennis. "The Politics of Choice: A View from the Bridge." In *Parents, Teachers and Children.* San Francisco: Institute for Contemporary Studies, 1977, p. 227.

Educational Economic Policy Center. *A New Accountability System for Texas Public Schools,* Vol. 1. Austin, TX: State of Texas, February 1993.

Educational Economic Policy Center. *Between Goals and Improvement: Sanctions and Rewards for Educational Results.* Public Policy Paper. Austin, TX: February 1993.

Elmore, R. F. *Choice in Public Education.* Center for Policy Research in Education, Rutgers University, 1986.

Elmore, R., and M. MacLaughlin. *Steady Work: Policy, Practice and the Reform of American Education.* Santa Monica, CA: RAND, 1988.

Elmore, Richard F. *Choice in Public Education.* Center for Policy Research in Education, Santa Monica, CA: RAND, December 1986.

Elmore, Richard F., and Associates. *Restructuring Schools: The Next Generation of Educational Reform.* San Francisco: Jossey-Bass Publishers, 1991.

Encarnation, Dennis J. "Public Finance and Regulation of Nonpublic Education: Retrospect and Prospect." *Public Dollars for Private Schools: The Case of Tuition Tax Credits,* Thomas James and

Henry M. Levin (eds.). Philadelphia: Temple University Press, 1983, pp. 175–195.

Farkas, Steve. *Divided Within, Besieged Without.* New York: The Public Agenda Foundation, 1993.

Finn, Chester E., Jr. "Reinventing Local Control." *Education Week,* January 23, 1991, pp. 32, 40.

Finn, Chester E., Jr. "What If Those Math Standards Are Wrong?" *Education Week,* January 30, 1993, p. 36.

Fisher, Roger, William Urey, and Bruce Patton. *Getting to Yes: Negotiating Agreement Without Giving In.* Boston: Houghton Mifflin, 1991.

Friedman, Milton. *Capitalism and Freedom.* Chicago: University of Chicago Press, 1962.

Fuhrman, Susan H., and Richard Elmore. "Understanding Local Control in the Wake of State Education Reform." *Educational Evaluation and Policy Analysis*, Vol. 12, Spring 1990, pp. 82–86.

Garkinkel, Irwin, and Edward Gramlick. *A Statistical Analysis of the OEO Experiment in Educational Performance Contracting.* Washington, D.C.: The Brookings Institution, Technical Service Reprint T-002, 1972.

Gemello, John M., and Jack W. Osman. "The Choice for Public and Private Education: An Economist's View." *Public Dollars for Private Schools: The Case of Tuition Tax Credits,* Thomas James and Henry M. Levin (eds.). Philadelphia: Temple University Press, 1983, pp. 196–209.

Glazer, Nathan. "The Future Under Tuition Tax Credits." *Public Dollars for Private Schools: The Case of Tuition Tax Credits,* Thomas James and Henry M. Levin (eds.). Philadelphia: Temple University Press, 1983, pp. 87–100.

Governor's Council on Education Reform and Funding. *Putting Children First: Improving Student Performance in Washington State.* Olympia, WA, 1993.

Grissmer, David, and Sheila Kirby. *Patterns of Attrition Among Indiana Teachers 1965–1987.* Santa Monica, CA: RAND, 1991.

Hannaway, J. "Political Pressure and Decentralization in Institutional Organizations: The Case of School Districts." *Sociology of Education,* Vol. 66, 1993.

Hannaway, J. "School Districts: The Missing Link in Education Reform." Stanford University. Paper prepared for the Association of Public Policy and Management Association Annual Meeting, Denver, CO, October 1992.

Hannaway, J., and L. Sproull. "Who's in Charge Here: Coordination and Control in Educational Organizations." *Administrators Notebook,* Vol. 27, 1977.

Harvey, James. *The Lake Union Statement: Reconciling Systemic Reform, Charters, and Contracting.* Seattle: University of Washington Graduate School of Public Affairs, working paper, 1994.

Hill, Paul T. "Urban Education." *Urban America: Policy Choices for Los Angeles and the Nation.* Santa Monica, CA: RAND, 1992, pp. 127–151.

Hill, Paul T., and Josephine Bonan. *Decentralization and Accountability in Public Education.* Santa Monica, CA: RAND, 1991.

Hill, Paul T., and Doren Madey. *Educational Policymaking Through the Civil Justice System.* Santa Monica, CA: RAND, 1982.

Hill, Paul T., Leslie Shapiro, and Arthur Wise. *Educational Progress: Cities Mobilize to Improve Their Schools.* Santa Monica, CA: RAND, 1989.

Hill, Paul T., Gail E. Foster, and Tamar Gendler. *High Schools with Character.* Santa Monica, CA: RAND, 1990.

Hirschman, Albert. *Exit, Voice and Loyalty: Responses to Decline in Firms and Organizations.* Cambridge, MA: Harvard University Press, 1969.

James, Thomas. "Questions About Educational Choice: An Argument from History." *Public Dollars for Private Schools: The Case of Tuition Tax Credits*, Thomas James and Henry M. Levin (eds.). Philadelphia: Temple University Press, 1983, pp. 55–70.

Jencks, Christopher. "Is the Public School Obsolete?" *The Public Interest*, Vol. 18, No. 2, Winter 1966.

Jencks, Christopher, and Judith Areen. *Education Vouchers: A Report on Financing Elementary Education by Grants to Parents.* Cambridge, MA: Center for the Study of Public Policy, 1970.

Jensen, Donald N. "Constitutional and Legal Implications of Tuition Tax Credits." *Public Dollars for Private Schools: The Case of Tuition Tax Credits*, Thomas James and Henry M. Levin (eds.). Philadelphia: Temple University Press, 1983, pp. 151–174.

Johnson, S. M. "Can Schools Be Reformed at the Bargaining Table? *Teachers College Record*, Vol. 89, No. 2, 1987, pp. 269–280.

Johnson, S. M. *Teacher Unions in Schools.* Philadelphia: Temple University Press, 1984.

Kearns, David T., and Denis P. Doyle. *Winning the Brain Race.* San Francisco: Institute for Contemporary Studies Press, 1988.

Kerchner, C. T. "Union-Made Teaching: The Effects of Labor Relations on Teaching Work." *Review of Research in Education 12*, E. Z. Rothkopf (ed.). Washington, D.C.: American Education Research Association, 1986.

Kimbrough, Jackie, and Paul T. Hill. *The Aggregate Effects of Federal Education Programs.* Santa Monica, CA: RAND, 1981.

Kirp, D., and D. Jensen. *School Days, Rule Days.* London: Falmer Press, 1986.

Kolderie, T. "School-Site Management: Rhetoric and Reality." Minneapolis: Humphrey Institute, University of Minnesota, 1988.

Kolderie, T. "The States Would Have to Withdraw the Exclusive." Minneapolis: University of Minnesota, Center for Policy Studies, 1992.

Koretz, Daniel M. "Educational Practices, Trends in Achievement, and the Potential of the Reform Movement," *Educational Administration Quarterly,* Vol. 24, No. 3, pp. 350–359, 1988.

Koretz, Daniel M. "The Effects of High Stakes Testing on Achievment: Preliminary Findings About Generalization Across Tests." Los Angeles: Center for Research on Evaluation, Standards, and Student Testing, 1991.

Kozol, Jonathan. *Savage Inequalities: Children in America's Schools.* New York: Harper Perennial, 1992.

Levin, Henry M. "Educational Choice and the Pains of Democracy." *Public Dollars for Private Schools: The Case of Tuition Tax Credits,* Thomas James and Henry M. Levin (eds.). Philadelphia: Temple University Press, 1983, pp. 17–38.

Levin, Henry. "The Failure of the Public Schools and the Free Market Remedy." *The Urban Review,* Vol. 32, No. 2, June 1968.

Lipsitz, J. *Successful Schools for Young Adolescents.* New Brunswick, NJ: Transaction Press, 1983.

Lipsky, M. *Street-Level Bureaucracy.* New York: Russell Sage Foundation, 1980.

Longanecker, David A. "The Public Cost of Tuition Tax Credits." *Public Dollars for Private Schools: The Case of Tuition Tax Credits,* Thomas James and Henry M. Levin (eds.). Philadelphia: Temple University Press, 1983, pp. 115–129.

Malen, B., and A. W. Hart. "Career Ladder Reform: A Multi-Level Analysis of Initial Efforts." *Educational Evaluation and Policy Analysis,* Vol. 9, No. 1, 1987, pp. 9–23.

March, James G., and Johan P. Olsen. *Rediscovering Institutions.* New York: Free Press, 1989.

McDonnell, Lorraine, and Paul T. Hill. *Newcomers in American Schools: Meeting the Educational Needs of Immigrant Youth.* Santa Monica, CA: RAND, 1993.

McDonnell, Lorraine, and Anthony Pascal. *Teacher Unions and Education Policy.* Santa Monica, CA: RAND, 1988.

Meyer, J. W., and B. Rowan. "The Structure of Education Organizations." *Environments and Organizations,* J. W. Meyer and Associates. San Francisco: Jossey-Bass, 1978.

Muller, Carol Blue. "The Social and Political Consequences of Increased Public Support for Private Schools." *Public Dollars for Private Schools: The Case of Tuition Tax Credits,* Thomas James and Henry M. Levin (eds.). Philadelphia: Temple University Press, 1983, pp. 39–54.

Murnane, Richard J. "Family Choice in Public Education: The Roles of Students, Teachers, and System Designers." *Teachers College Record,* Vol. 88, No. 2, Winter 1986.

Murnane, Richard J. "The Uncertain Consequences of Tuition Tax Credits: An Analysis of Student Achievement and Economic Incentives." *Public Dollars for Private Schools: The Case of Tuition Tax Credits,* Thomas James and Henry M. Levin (eds.). Philadelphia: Temple University Press, 1983, pp. 210–222.

Nathan, Joe. *Public Schools by Choice: Expanding Opportunities for Parents, Students, and Teachers.* Bloomington, IN: Meyer Share Books, 1989.

O'Day, Jennifer, and Marshall S. Smith. "Systemic School Reform and Educational Opportunity." Stanford University School of Education, September 24, 1992.

Osborne, David, and Ted Gaebler, *Reinventing Government.* Menlo Park, CA: Addison-Wesley, 1992.

Powell, Arthur, Eleanor Farrar, and David Cohen. *The Shopping Mall High School: Winners and Losers in the Educational Marketplace.* Boston: Houghton-Mifflin, 1985.

Purkey, Stewart, and Marshall Smith. "Effective Schools: A Review." *Elementary School Journal,* Vol. 83, No. 4, 1983, pp. 427–451.

Raywid, M. A. "Family Choice Arrangements in Public Schools: A Review of the Literature." *Review of Educational Research,* Vol. 55, No. 4, 1985, pp. 435–467.

Rosenholtz, S. J. "Effective Schools: Interpreting the Evidence." *American Journal of Education*, Vol. 93, No. 3, 1984, pp. 352–388.

Senge, Peter. *The Fifth Discipline.* New York: Currency Doubleday, 1990.

Shanker, Albert. "A Proposal for Using Incentives to Restructure Our Public Schools." *Phi Delta Kappan*, Vol. 71, No. 5, January 1990, pp. 344–357.

Sherman, Joel D. "Public Finance of Private Schools: Observations from Abroad." *Public Dollars for Private Schools: The Case of Tuition Tax Credits*, Thomas James and Henry M. Levin (eds.). Philadelphia: Temple University Press, 1983, pp. 71–86.

Shires, Michael A., Cathy S. Krop, C. Peter Rydell, and Stephen J. Carroll. *The Effects of the California Voucher Initiative on Public Expenditures for Education.* Santa Monica, CA: RAND, 1994.

Sizer, Theodore. *Horace's Compromise: The Dilemma of the American High School.* Boston: Houghton-Mifflin, 1984.

Smith, Marshall S. "A National Curriculum in the United States?" *Education Leadership*, Vol. 49, No. 1, pp. 74–81.

Smith, Marshall S., and Jennifer O'Day. "Systemic School Reform." *The Politics of Curriculum and Testing*, Susan Fuhrman and Betty Malen (eds.). Bristol, PA: The Falmer Press, 1991.

Tyack, David, and Thomas James. "State Government and American Public Education: Exploring the Primeval Forest." *History of Education Quarterly*, Vol. 26, No. 1, Spring 1986.

Tyack, David. "Restructuring in Historical Perspective: Tinkering Toward Utopia." *Teachers College Record*, Vol. 92, No. 2, Winter 1990, pp. 170–191.

Tyack, David. *The One Best System, A History of American Urban Education.* Cambridge, MA: Harvard University Press, 1974.

Willms, J. Douglas. "Do Private Schools Produce Higher Levels of Academic Achievement? New Evidence for the Tuition Tax Credit Debate." *Public Dollars for Private Schools: The Case of Tuition*

Tax Credits, Thomas James and Henry M. Levin (eds.).   Philadelphia: Temple University Press, 1983, pp. 223–234.

Wise, Arthur E. *Legislated Learning.* Berkeley, CA: University of California Press, 1979.

Wise, Arthur E. *Rich Schools Poor Schools.* Chicago: University of Chicago Press, 1968.